Tilly and Elmer

The Sexy Seniors of South Branch Coloring Book

for Grown-ups

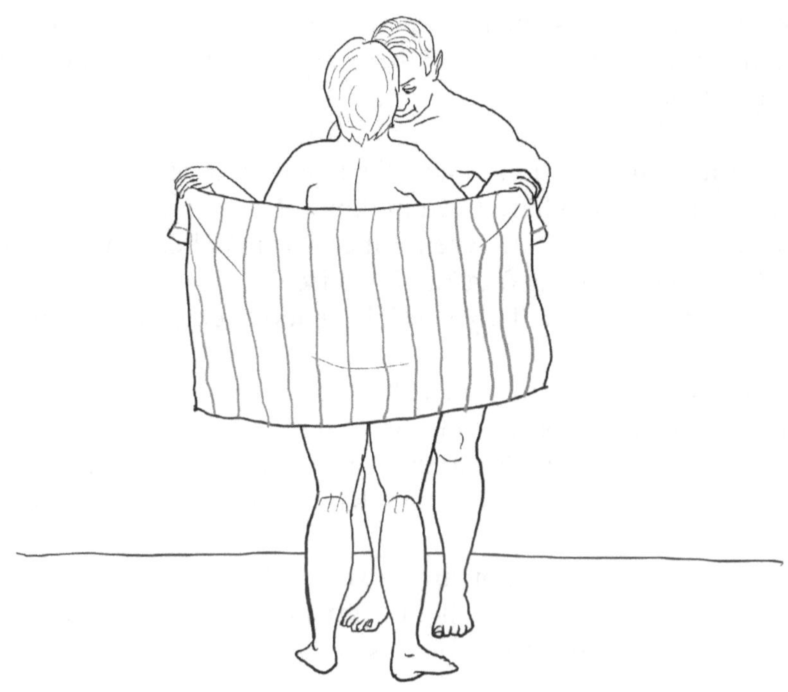

Written and Illustrated by

Gene Clements

Pickleworks Press
Zesty Dill Editions

ISBN-10: 0-9962827-2-6
ISBN-13: 978-0-9962827-2-7

TillyandElmer.com
PickleworksPress.com

About Tilly and Elmer

The drawings in this book are based on a selection of illustrations from the short stories which make up the series called ***The Sexy Seniors of South Branch***. Tilly and Elmer are a frisky Midwestern couple in their late sixties. They've been married for close to fifty years, they still really like each other, and they know what to do about it.

The pair would appear to the casual observer to be the definition of an "old married couple"; but while they ARE a couple, AND married, they don't consider themselves OLD. In fact, they still feel like teenagers most of the time, although sometimes events remind them that they aren't quite as athletic, skinny, or flexible as they were five decades ago. No matter. They try to recapture their youth anyway; and when they can't quite recapture it, they at least give it a good chase. Along the way, they have some fun and get themselves into, and usually out of, some humorous situations. What they've lost over the years in body tone, they have gained in expertise, imagination, and good humor.

Tilly and Elmer live on a small farm near the made-up town of South Branch, Iowa. They were high school sweethearts and have lived in South Branch all their lives, except, of course, during the four years in the mid 1960's when Elmer was in college in Cedar Falls and Tilly was studying nursing (among other things) in San Francisco.

That's another story, but so far, Tilly hasn't been too keen on letting me write it.

The entire collection of Tilly and Elmer short stories, including all fifty illustrations, is available in paperback at CreateSpace, Amazon, and elsewhere. Individual stories, as well as the collection, are available for any e-reader at the Amazon Kindle store, the Apple iBook store, Smashwords, the Barnes and Noble Nook store, Kobo, and other on line e-book retailers.

A companion series and a corresponding novel, ***Tilly and Elmer FlashbackX - Coming of Age in South Branch***, about their high school courtship in rural Iowa in the early 1960's can be found in paperback as well as all e-book formats at the same sources.

I hope coloring book fans are delighted by the antics of Tilly and Elmer and enjoy applying their creative talents to making them the colorful characters they are. So, even if it's not time for your 50th high school reunion or you don't have a creek suitable for skinny-dipping, get out your favorite coloring tools and party along with Tilly and Elmer.

Acknowledgments

A Tilly and Elmer Coloring Book! Who would have thought it would come to this? I have to thank Judy Logan for giving me the idea and my coffee-drinking buddies for failing to dissuade me in the endeavor. Elizabeth Johnson's skillful editing and sound advice were invaluable as always.

As usual, my wife Ann encouraged me to take up this project and I always appreciate her enthusiasm for my Tilly and Elmer schemes.

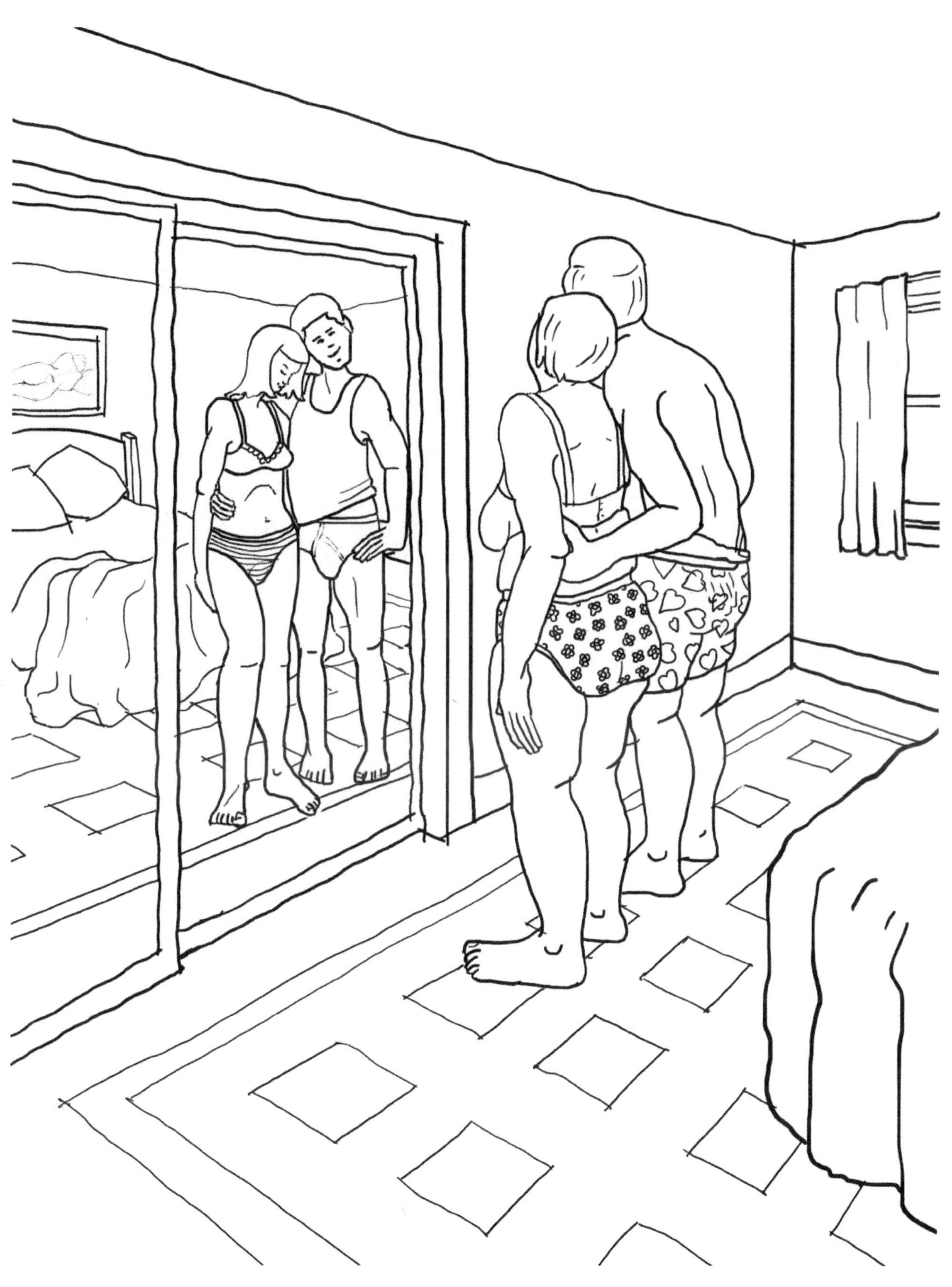

"You still look just as good as you did back in high school, Tilly!"
"You're only saying that so you can get into my pants, Elmer. Of course it still works every time!"

Tilly and Elmer - The Sexy Seniors of South Branch

The illustrations on the facing pages are from a series of short stories recounting the frisky adventures of Tilly and Elmer, a long married couple from rural Iowa. On the following pages you'll find thirty of the fifty illustrations from the book ***The Sexy Seniors of South Branch*** plus a few that are new in this book.

Each story is introduced with a short description, and each drawing includes a quote from the book and is labeled with the short story it comes from at the top of the page.

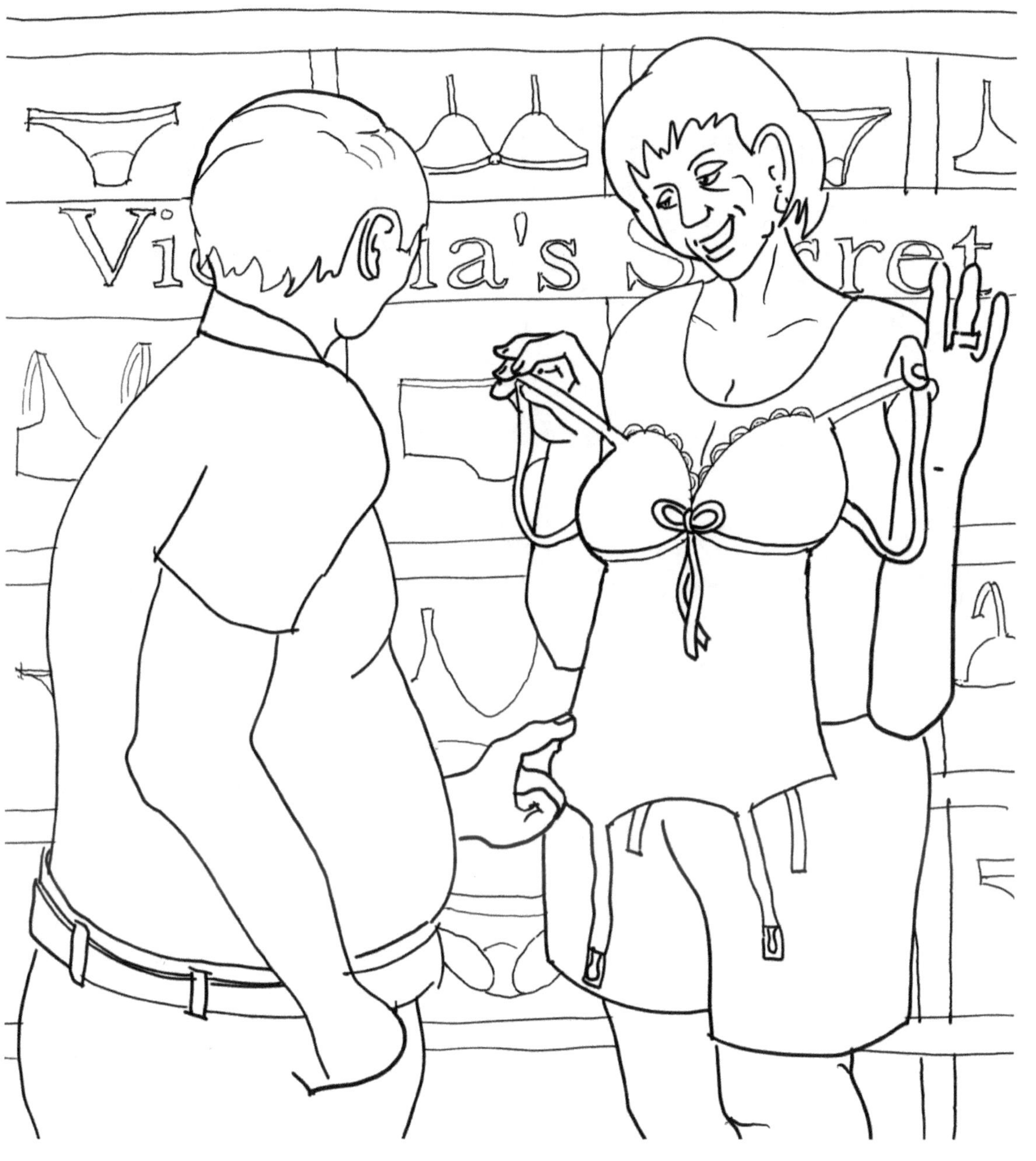

"Take a look at this corset, Elmer? Does it do anything for you?"
"It's turning me on and you aren't even wearing it yet! It's almost as exciting as those baby doll pajamas you were wearing that night at the Sleeptite Motel fifty years ago."
"Those did something for you all right, back in the day!"
"They sure did Tilly, and do you know what I liked best about them?"
"No, what?"
"I liked the way they looked draped over the back of the chair!"

Tilly and Elmer Get Crazy

As soon as Tilly pulls the latest issue of *Women's Excitement* magazine out of her shopping bag, and begins to read the romantic advice article, "Four Ways to Drive your Man Crazy in the Bedroom", she and Elmer are propelled unexpectedly into a shocking mélange of dancing and Dr. Pepper, melon balls and bacon, panties and peacock feathers, corsets and dog collars. In the end, they each succeed in driving the other crazy, but they have fun on the way, and so will the reader.

Critics have called this episode the best "Tilly and Elmer" since the last "Tilly and Elmer". High praise indeed!

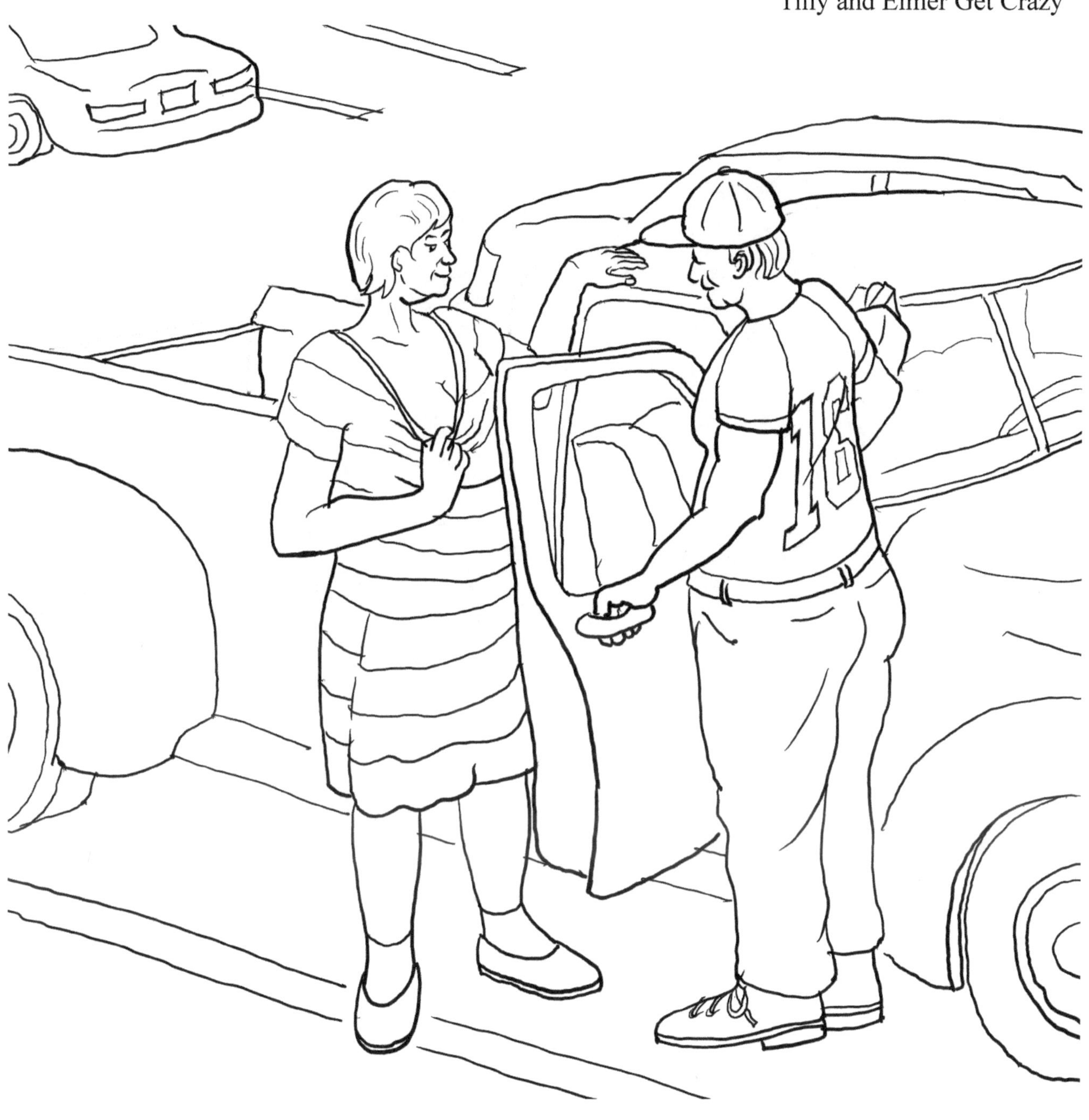

"I got you new batteries for your hearing aid," Tilly said, as they started home from town in Elmer's old pickup.

"What?" replied Elmer.

Tilly just smiled as she took her new magazine, *Woman's Excitement*, out of the grocery bag. As usual, the cover promised romantic advice. This month it was, "Four Ways to Drive your Man Crazy in the Bedroom." Tilly wondered if it also included instructions on keeping him from being crazy the rest of the time.

"Listen to this, Elmer," she said, "Here's an article on how I can drive you crazy in bed!"

"You already drive me crazy in bed Tilly!" said Elmer with a grin. "Like when you mention that the bedroom ceiling needs painting just when I'm about to finish making love to you."

"Not crazy that way, silly," said Tilly. "I mean how to make you wildly sexually excited!"

"What does it recommend?" asked Elmer.

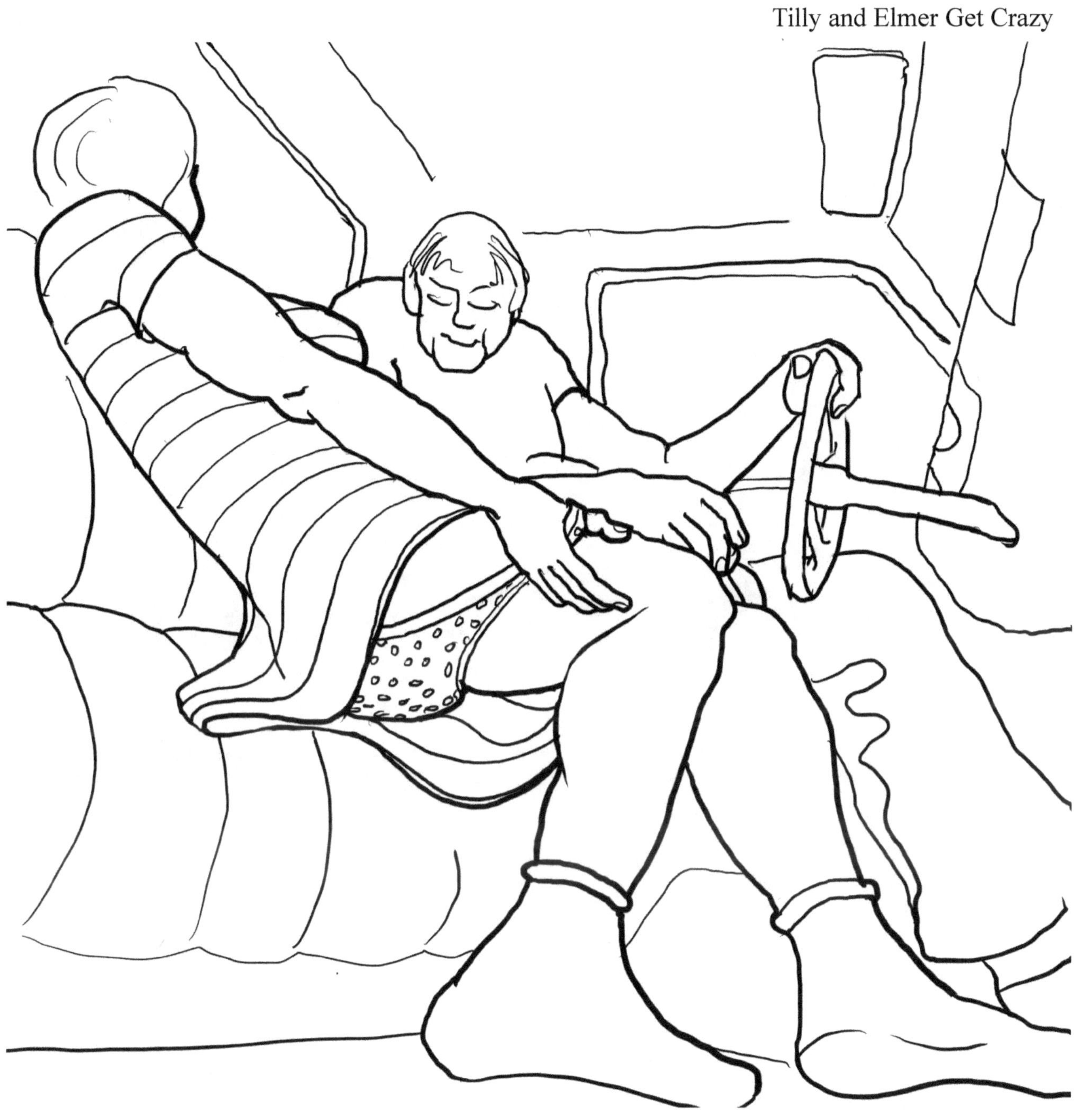

"Tip Number 1, Do What he Loved When You Were First Dating"

"I'll SHOW you!" laughed Tilly as they reached the railroad tracks at the edge of town. She raised her bottom off the seat, pulled up her dress, and slipped off her panties. Elmer was beginning to like this article.

"I thought you said, 'Drive your man crazy in bed,' not 'bed your man while he's driving.' "

"You didn't see anything dangerous about it when we were eighteen," Tilly laughed.

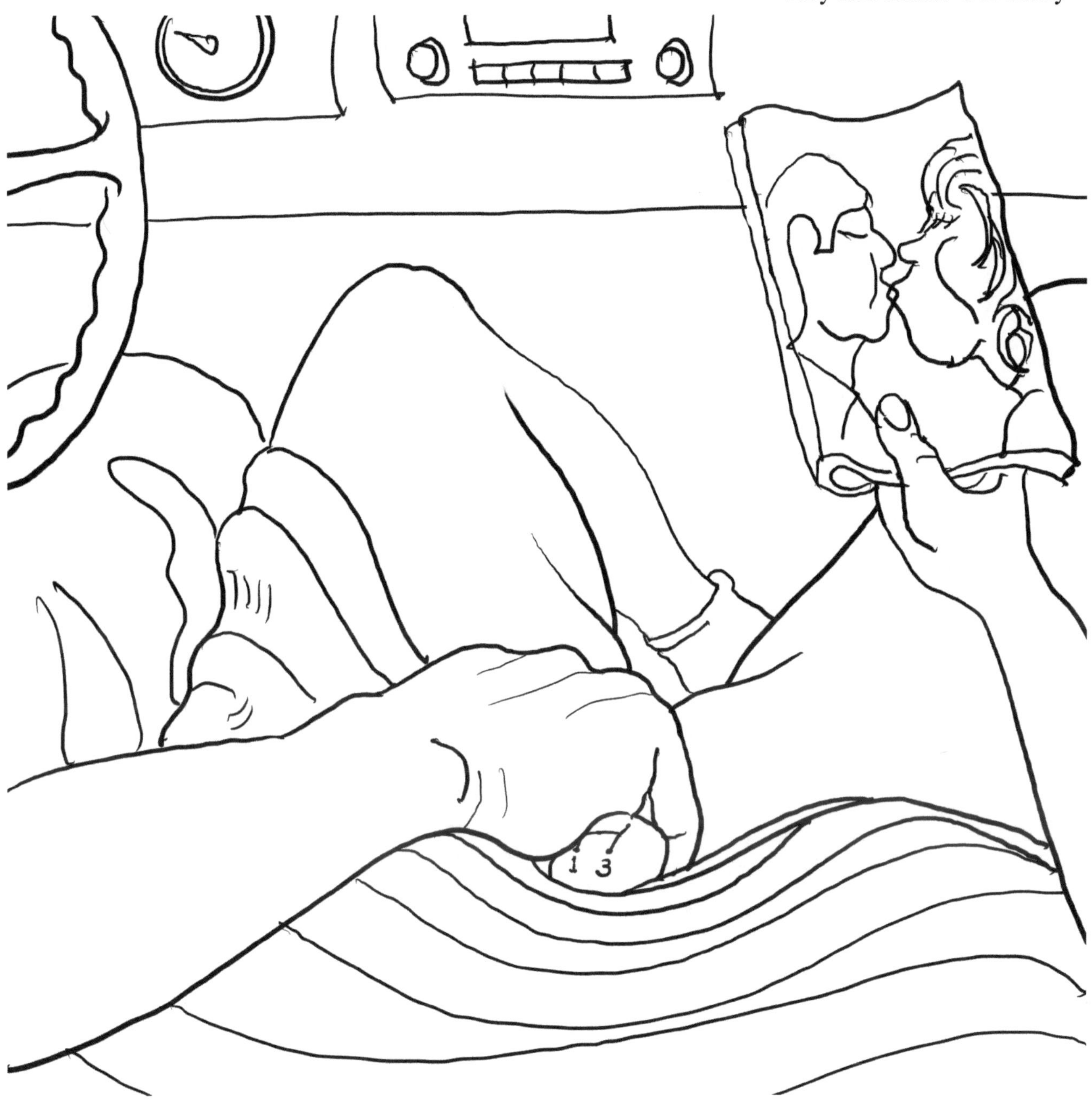

Tilly slid over next to Elmer and put her hand on his thigh. The restored truck, the same one Elmer had when they were dating, had a manual transmission with the shift lever on the floor. Tilly straddled the shift knob, just like she used to do, so that Elmer's hand was between her legs whenever he had to shift into first or third. It seemed to her that he had to shift more often when they were dating, but the lever still vibrated just like it always did which made each gear change even more fun for her.

"What do you say to taking the long way home and pulling over behind Old Man Smith's hedgerow like we used to?" said Elmer.

"No, it wouldn't be proper," said Tilly. "And besides, I have to get the milk, eggs, and bacon into the fridge before they spoil."

"It wasn't 'proper' then either," replied Elmer, "but I didn't notice that stopping us.

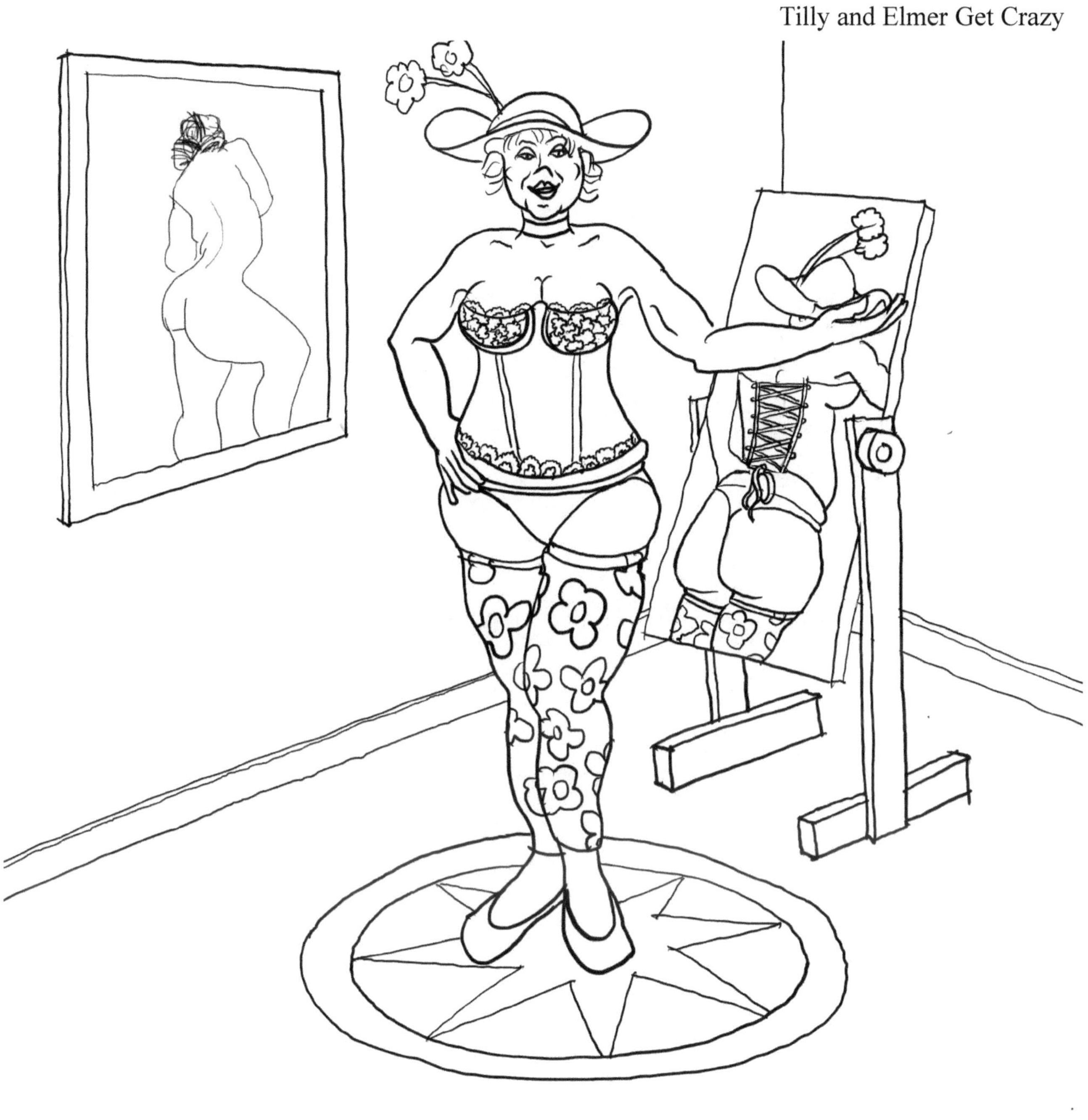

"Tip Number 2, Try a new look!"

Tilly modeled her creative fashion statement. The centerpiece of the outfit was a lacy corset she had found in an old trunk in the closet. Faded pink in color, it laced up the back. It was a bit wider in fit now than it was when she last wore it forty years ago, but it had driven him crazy then, and was a good start this time. On her head, Tilly wore a straw hat with a peacock feather that she had gotten from her grandmother. Around her neck was a leather collar that normally belonged to their dog, Alex. For her midsection, she had chosen thong underwear. She wore dark flowered tights with the top portion cut off to make leggings reaching to the tops of her thighs. On her feet were bobby socks and patent leather flats.

Elmer was speechless; she had all his favorites on at the same time. He revealed that her plan had worked and suggested they climb into bed.

"Not yet!" said Tilly. "You aren't crazy enough."

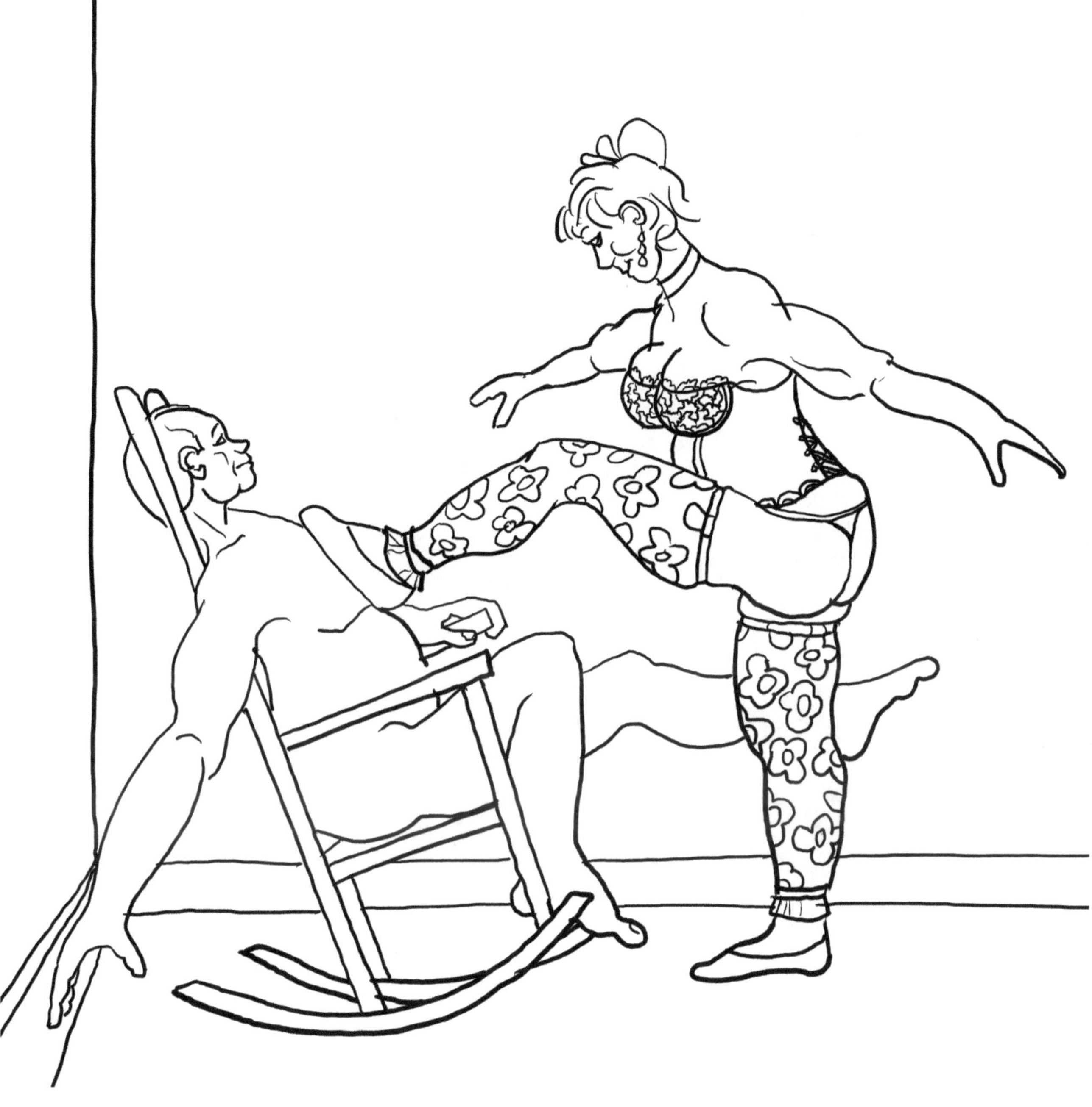

"Tip Number 3, Let go of Your Inhibitions and Dance for Him!"

Tilly wasn't known for her dancing, but she seemed to have gotten into the spirit of the article. She required Elmer to disrobe and settle back into the rocking chair they kept in the bedroom before beginning her performance. The dance included a number of moves involving undulating breasts quite near Elmer's face and hula-like shimmying of Tilly's bottom. She incorporated quite a few slow, loving, touches of Elmer's body, which did seem to have the effect of diminishing his sanity. He doubted Tilly could find work in the erotic dance field, but her performance was having the desired effect on him, that was for sure.

"That article was pretty accurate," whispered Elmer. "I believe you'll find me sufficiently crazy at this point."

"I'm just getting started, lover boy!" smiled Tilly.

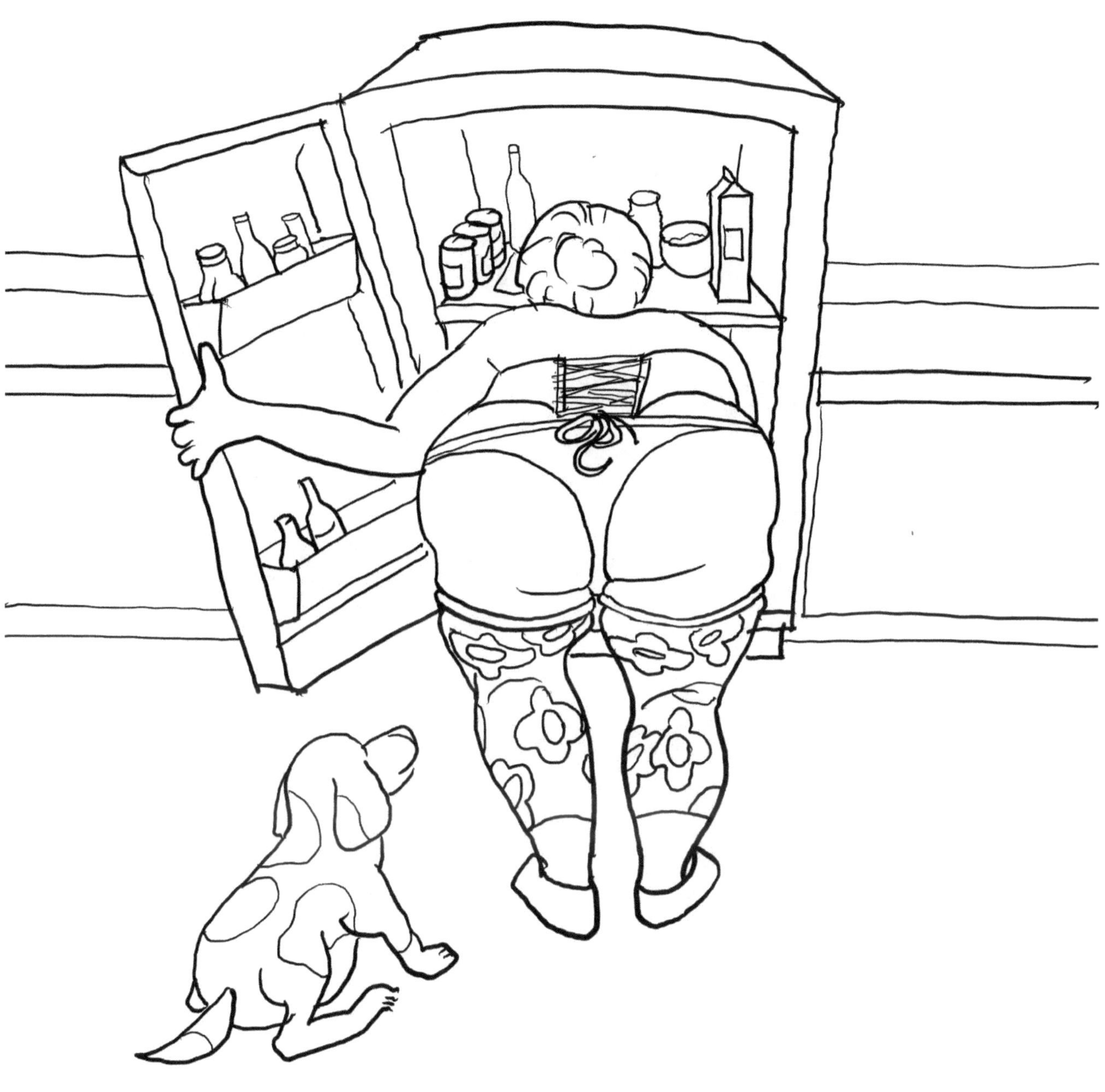

"Tip Number 4, Slip Something Sweet Into his Mouth!"

"DAMMIT!" said Tilly.
"What's the matter?"
"I forgot the melon balls."
"Forget the MELON balls!" advised Elmer. "I have two balls right here that are about to burst!"
"No, I have to follow the instructions if I'm going to drive you crazy!" Tilly got up and went into the kitchen. Elmer followed. Alex gave out a howl.
"Is she driving you crazy too?" Elmer asked him.

Tilly opened the refrigerator and bent over to retrieve the forgotten melon.
"She still has the world's cutest butt," Elmer thought.

Tilly and Elmer Get Warmed Up

Move over Dr. Zhivago. Step aside, Boris Pasternak. Don't even think about it, Omar Sharif.

Unknown author, Gene Clements, has created a frigid love story covering fifty years of romantic hardships, set against harsh Midwestern winters and bruised by lumpy, snow covered woodlands. You'll smile as the young Matilda cleverly ensnares a teenaged Elmer in a web of sexual desire, gasp as she nearly freezes to death as the result of a clumsy romantic gesture, blush as it's revealed who else knows his secret, recoil at his heartbreaking attempt, a half century later, to reprise a lifelong yearning, and find your spirits lifted (especially if you have a stiff drink in hand) by the story's touching climax.

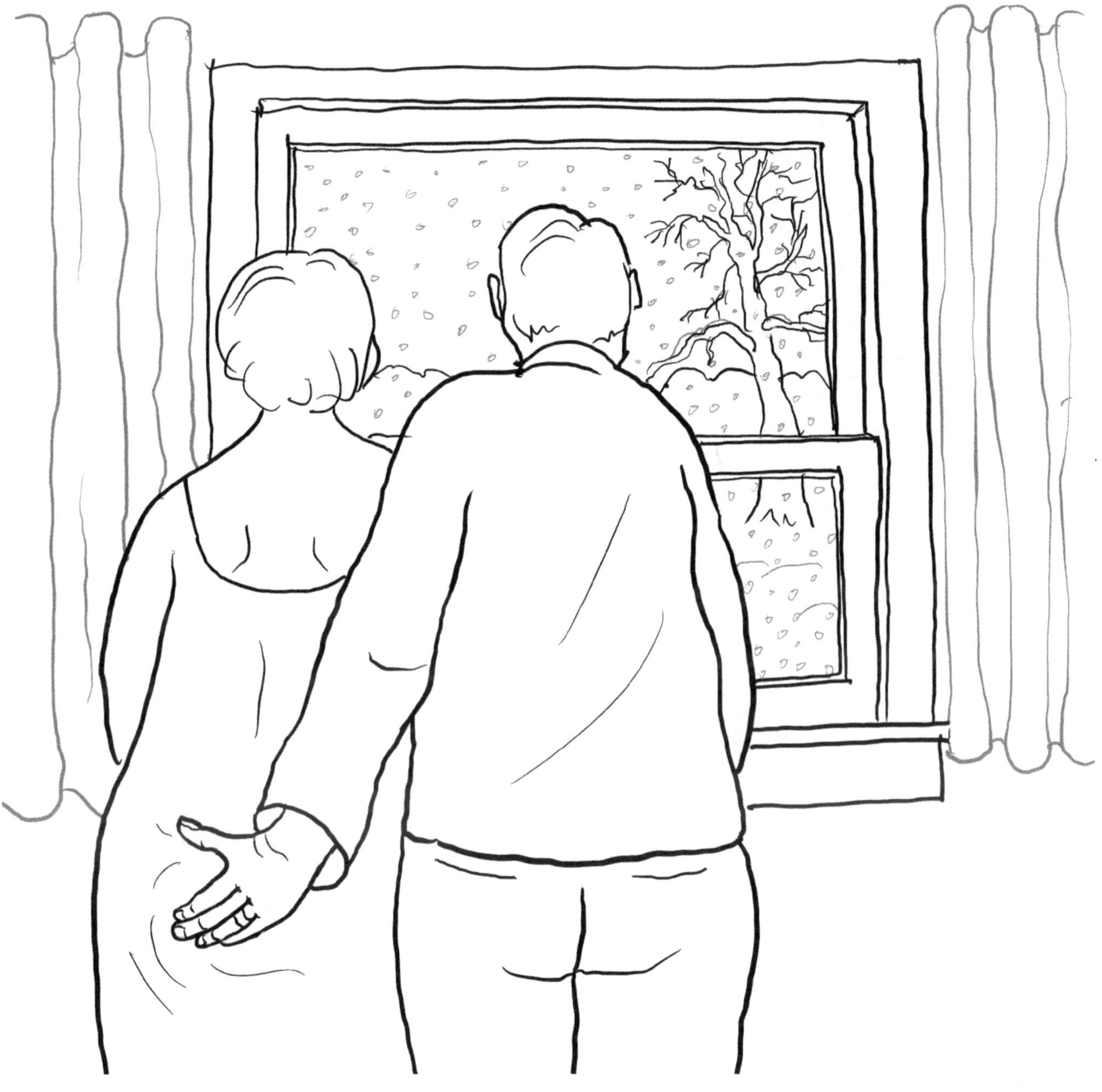

"Tilly, remember fifty years ago, before we were married and —"

"I think we both remember fifty years and fifty pounds ago, yes," laughed Tilly.

"— and that time we went out into the woods when it was snowy like this?" continued Elmer.

Tilly raised her left eyebrow. "You're not suggesting we —?"

"Sure I am. We haven't made love in the woods for years, especially not in the winter. We're always saying we should get out of our routine."

Tilly looked at him doubtfully. "Do you mean our routine of not freezing to death?"

"We didn't freeze to death that time. In fact I don't remember feeling the cold at all. It was pretty hot as I recall!" said Elmer.

Tilly gave him a little smile.

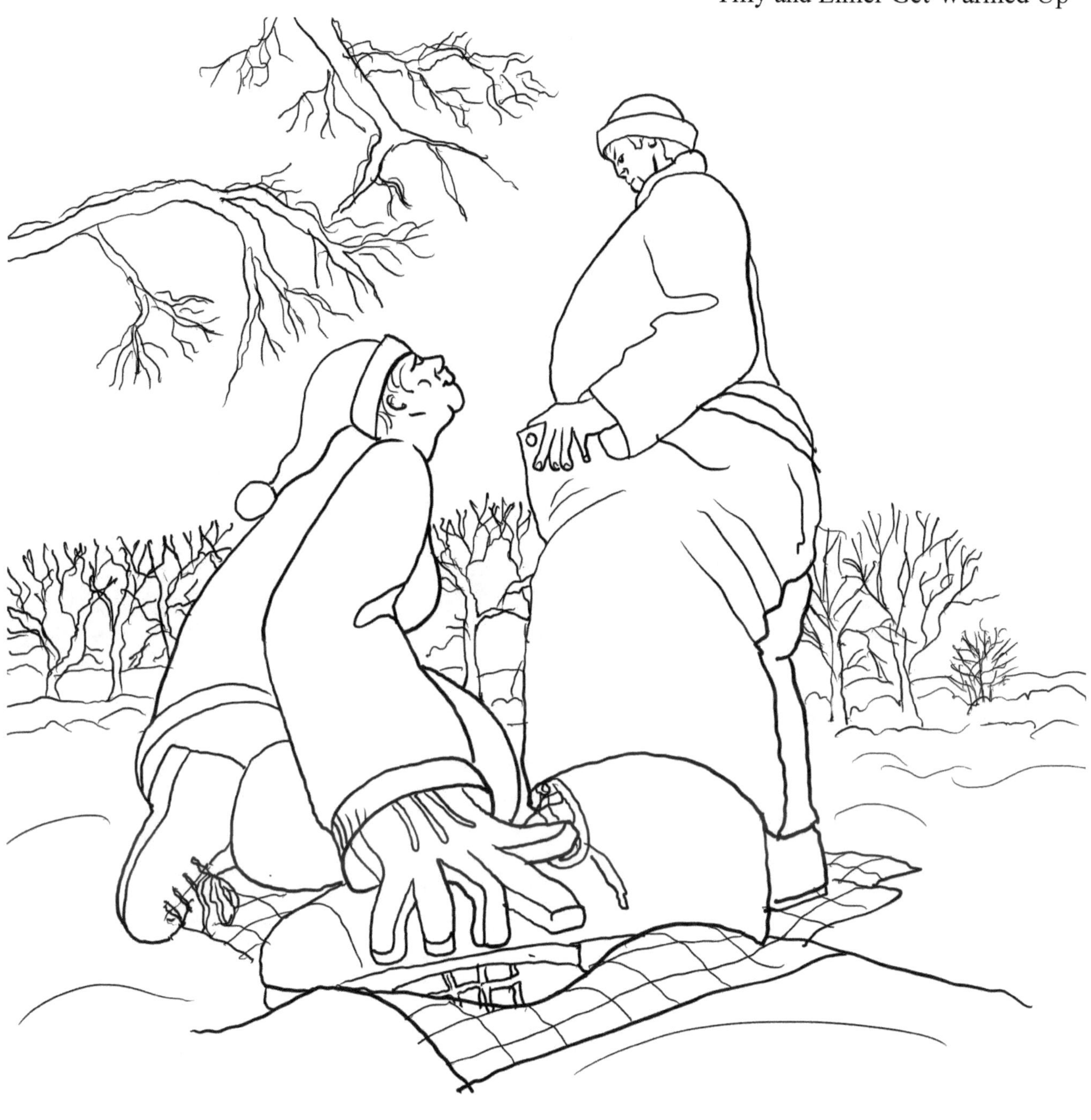

They found a spot behind a fallen tree, out of view of the new houses nearby, but there was no sun there.

"It will have to do," said Elmer.

"Ouch. There's a branch under me," said Tilly.

In fact, there were many branches and rocks under the only spot Tilly felt was sufficiently out of sight of the neighbors. After some effort they found a way to arrange themselves, but it wasn't exactly cozy. Elmer stood up, unzipped his fly, and lowered his long johns a few inches.

"I guess it's pretty cold out here!" observed Tilly. Elmer's manhood was the size of a cocktail weenie.

"What's the matter, big boy?" smiled Tilly. "You don't look quite as ready as you did at eighteen!"

"I'm ready, but apparently the telegraph wires are down because of the cold. The message doesn't seem to have gone through."

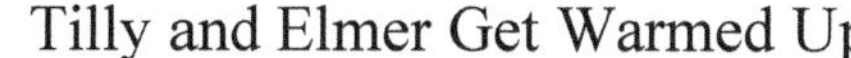

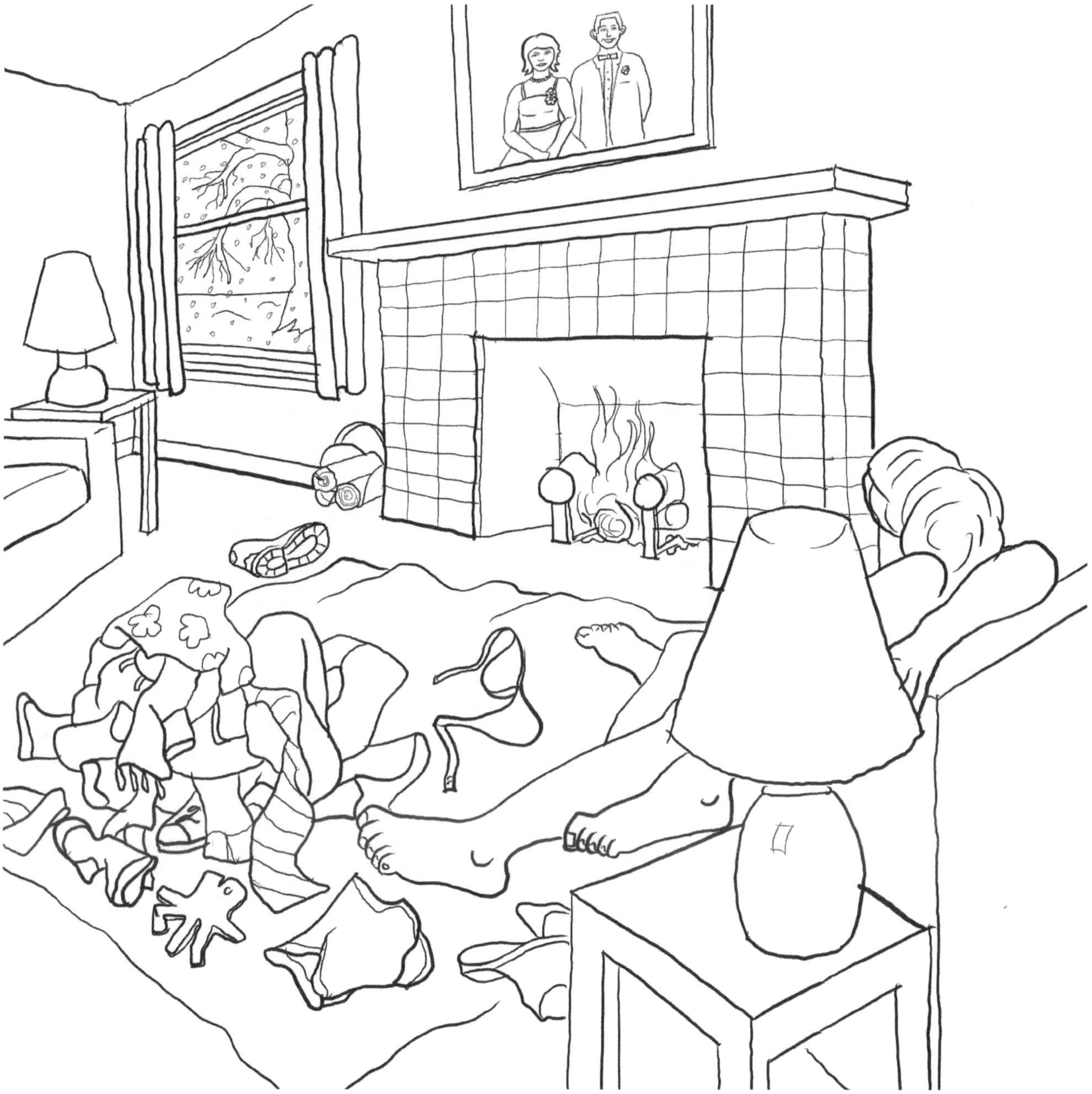

"I have an idea, Elmer," Tilly said.

"Does it involve getting warm?"

"Probably more than warm! You know that big, white, down comforter we have in the closet. The one that's so thick and soft?" asked Tilly.

"Yes."

"Let's go back to the house, spread it out in front of the fireplace, and pretend it's snow!"

Elmer gave her a hug. "You're a genius," he said.

Elmer built a fire and they sat on the floor, leaning back on the sofa as they sipped brandy, gradually warmed up, and eased out of their winter clothing. Elmer stood up so Tilly could pull off the last of his layers.

"Hey, it looks like the message has gotten through!" she laughed, giving Elmer a kiss on his belly.

Tilly and Elmer Go to Las Vegas

And Now … Soon to be a major motion picture ...
What the critics are saying:

"Except for the first paragraph, I couldn't understand a word of it. And what's a carburetor?" - MC

"This man is sick!" - Dr. P

"The best 'Tilly and Elmer' I've ever read..." - BO

"I'm thinking of sending the author my Nobel Prize ... but not the money." - AM

"I couldn't stop crying..." - JB

"Pure trash. An example of what's wrong with America..." - JD

"If I had read this as a young man, Mickey would have been a lot more fun." - WD

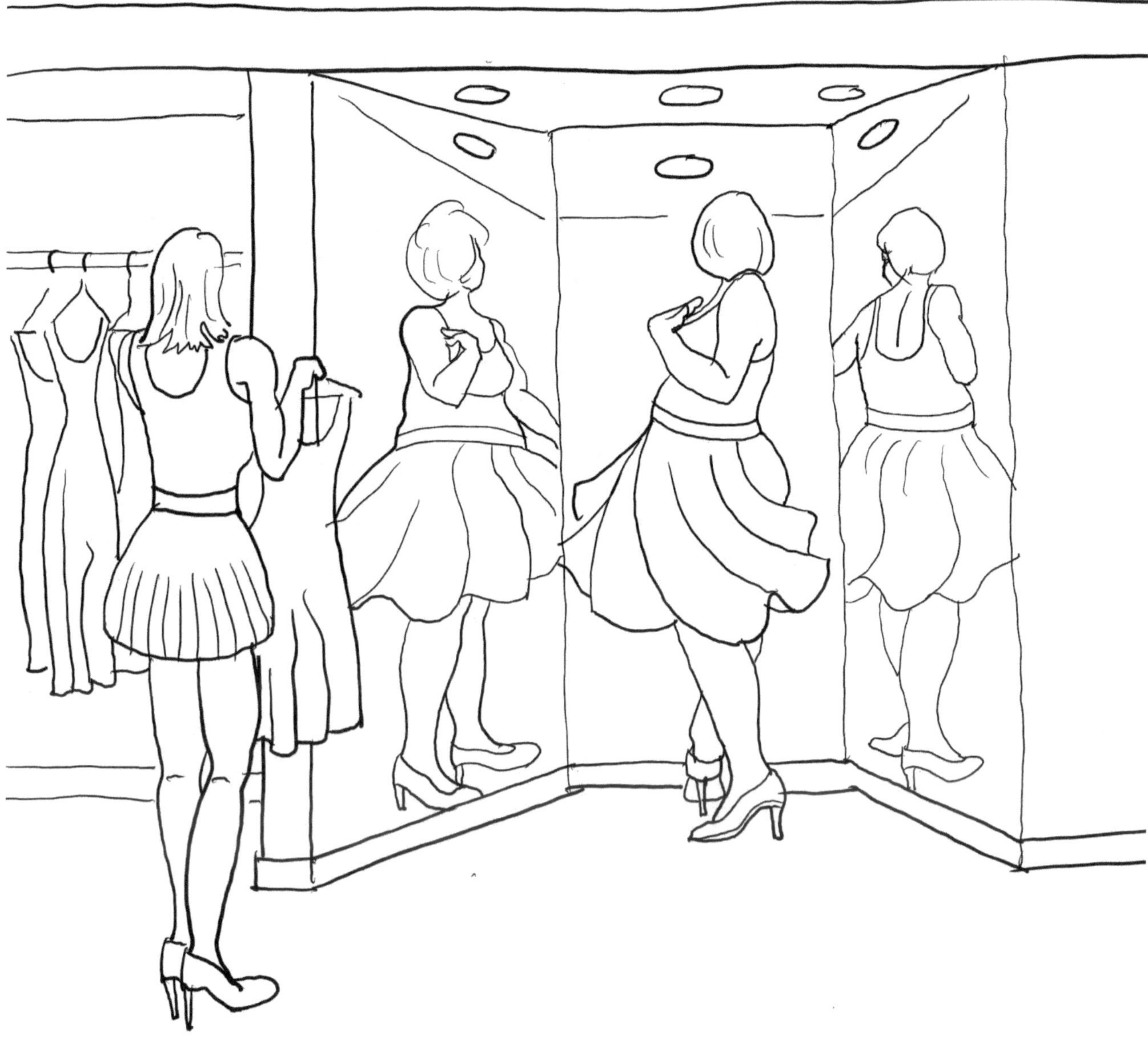

"I'm not going into that fancy restaurant in this old dress," she announced.

Before Elmer could protest, his eye was caught by a sparkly red dress in the window.

"Tilly would look nice in that!" he thought.

The red dress didn't appeal to Tilly, but after trying on several party dresses, a process that Elmer complained about, but secretly enjoyed, she chose a black silky top and matching skirt that flowed around her legs like bourbon appears to flow around your glass in slow motion when you've had one too many. She looked beautiful.

"I must say, Tilly, you'll give those eighty-year-old showgirls some pretty stiff competition in that dress."

"And I'm counting on you to give me something stiff once I get out of it," purred Tilly.

"Besides a drink, you mean?" chuckled Elmer.

"In addition to a drink!" whispered Tilly into his good ear.

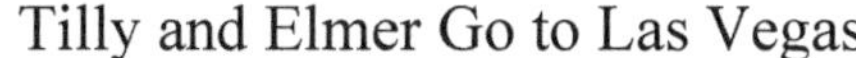

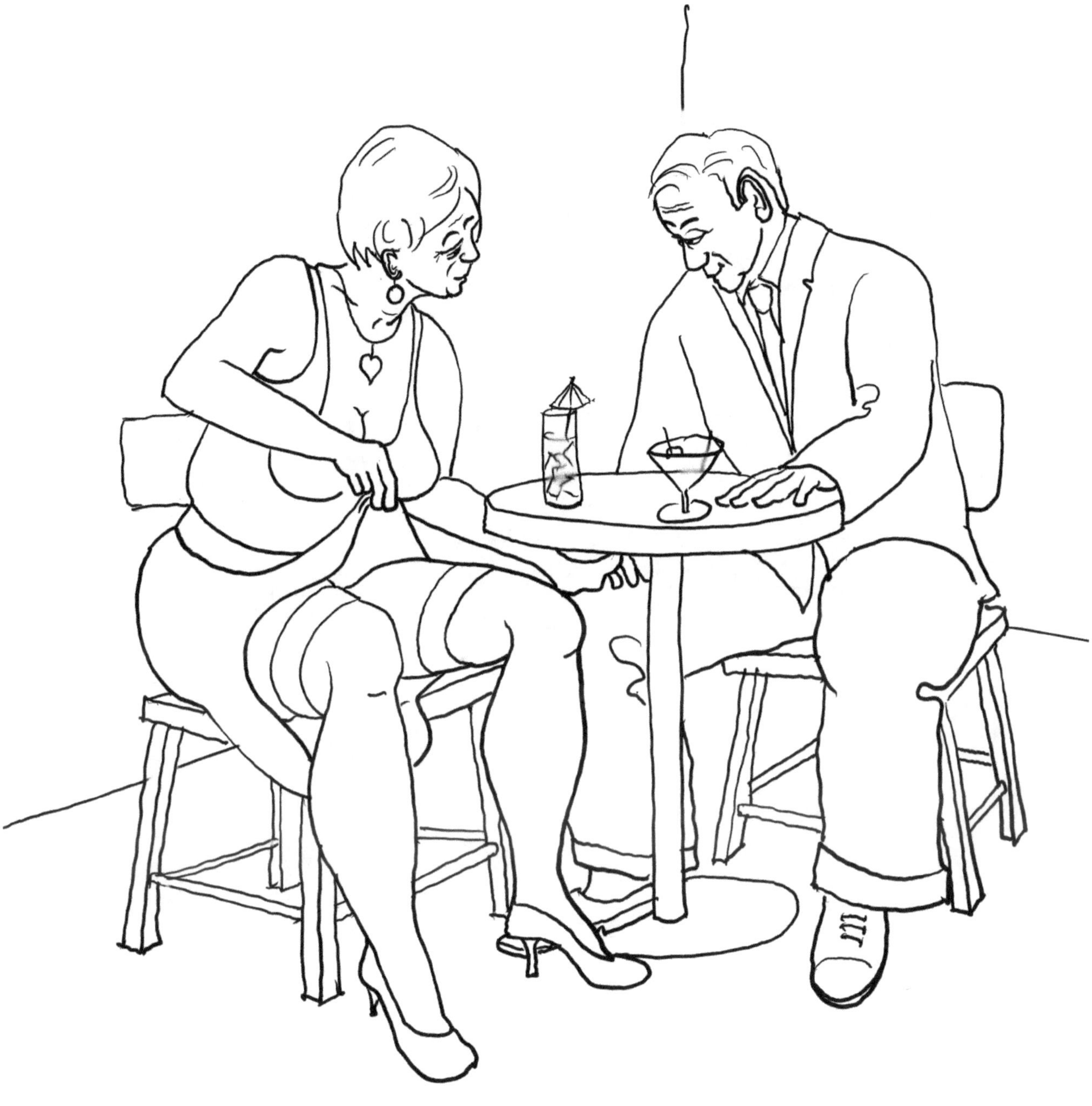

They got to the restaurant a little early and decided to wait in the bar until their table was ready, choosing a hideaway in the darkest corner.

As Elmer was pulling out Tilly's chair, she leaned over and said in a low voice, "Just in the interest of full disclosure, I'm not wearing any panties."

Elmer's jaw dropped. He'd always imagined her going out in public sans underwear, but she'd never done it before as far as he could remember, and he was pretty sure he would have remembered such an occasion. Elmer was a little distracted when the waitress came to take their order. He decided to celebrate the news with a double Martini.

Tilly had some kind of drink that was bright blue. As they were enjoying the drinks, she reached under the table and took Elmer's hand, then lifted the hem of her skirt to give him a little preview of what was to come. It was too dark to see any detail, and since the bar was crowded, Elmer decided against trying to use braille to verify Tilly's assertion, but he definitely was looking forward to the rest of the evening.

Tilly and Elmer's 50th Class Reunion

The newest blockbuster from soon to be unheralded author, Gene Clements. *Tilly and Elmer go to Their Fiftieth High School Reunion* is the vast and complex tale of a bitter fifty year rivalry that suddenly erupts in an explosion of shocking facial expressions, of unfulfilled dreams lost, and weight gained. A thrilling story of foreplay under the moonlight and carnal lust imagined under cool white fluorescent lighting.

You'll thrill to the clumsy drawings and inept writing of what critics have called the author's best work since "What I Liked Best About our Field Trip to the Chuckles Candy Factory" from fourth grade. So find a comfy chair, fix yourself a tall gin and tonic, and settle in for three minutes of the best reading you've experienced since you pitched out the junk mail a few minutes ago.

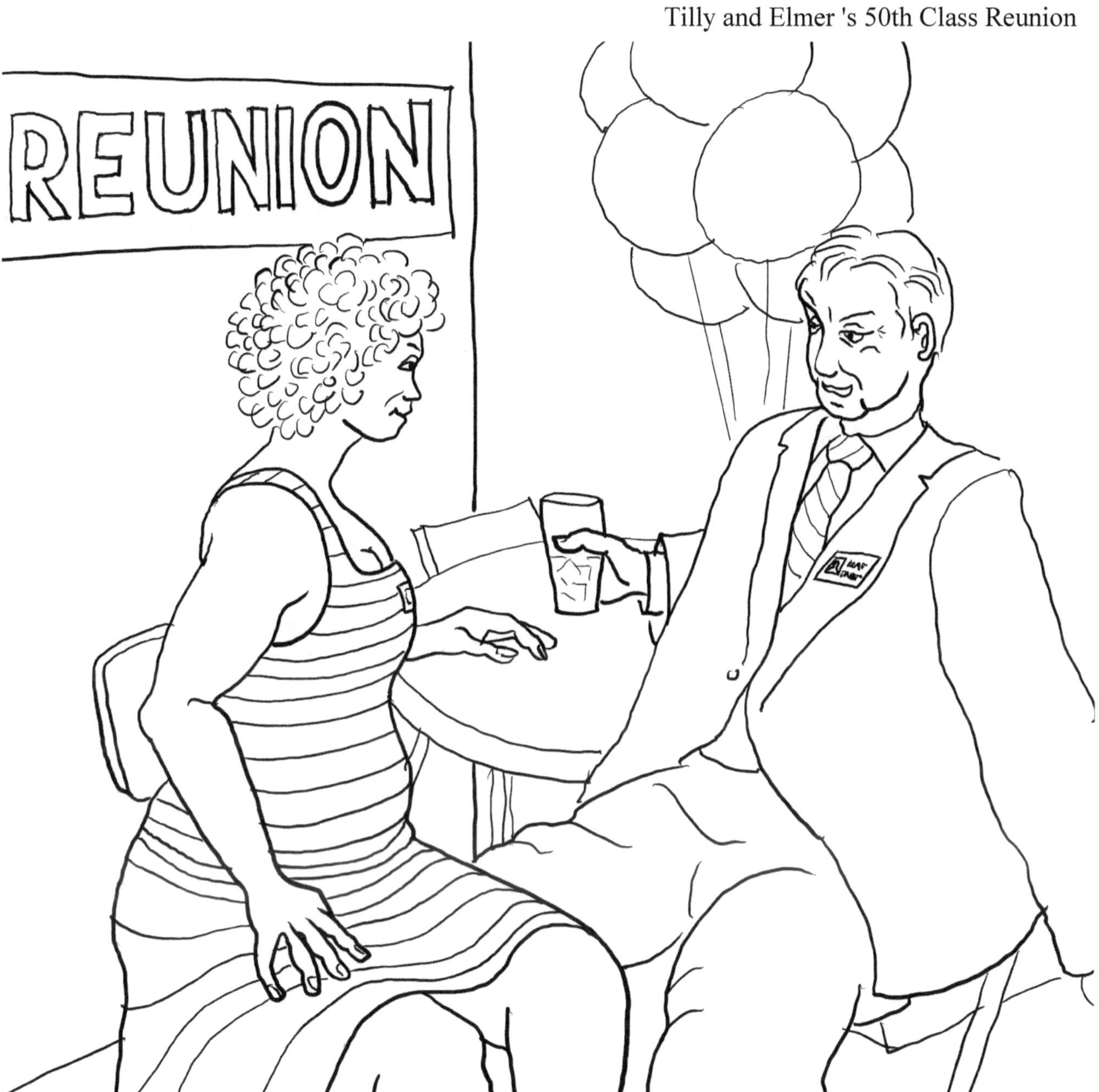

Susan remarked in passing that she always wondered, back then, why Elmer never asked her for a date, speculating that he must have had a girlfriend he never mentioned. She thought the comment was unremarkable; Elmer was speechless. He let her continue making small talk for a minute while he collected his wits. He had a girlfriend he never mentioned all right!

"Susan, are you telling me you would have gone out with me if I had asked?"

"Of course, why wouldn't I? You were SO smart and funny! I had a little crush on you back then; didn't you know?"

Elmer wasn't sure whether to laugh or cry so he just sat there for a minute looking at her, his mouth agape.

"Elmer, what are you thinking?" she asked softly, guessing correctly by the look on Elmer's face the general outline of his thoughts.

"I'm thinking I could use another gin and tonic."

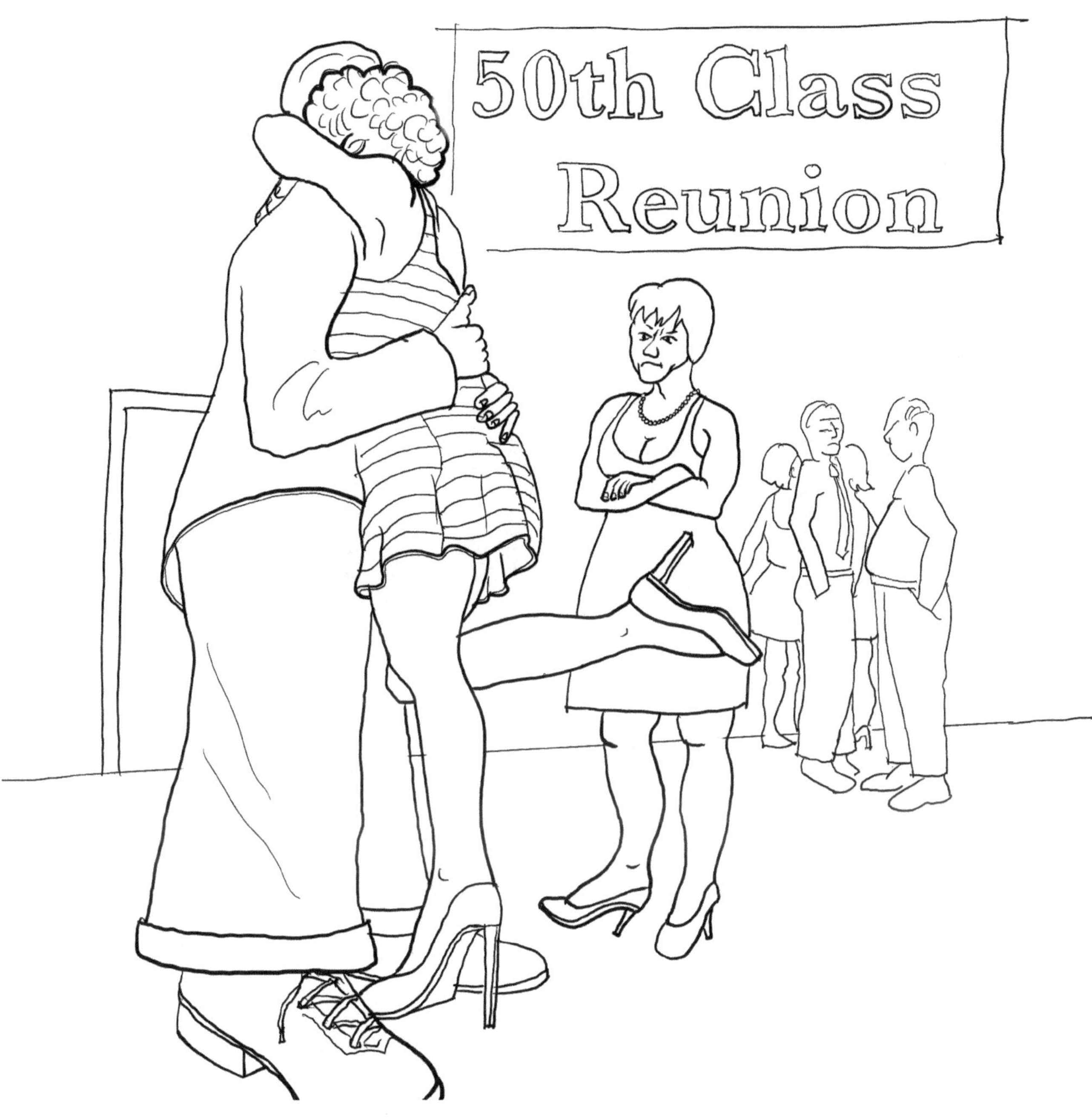

As they were leaving, Susan and Elmer gave each other a parting hug, the duration of which was much longer than Tilly thought absolutely necessary. Tilly pointed out Buff, arm in arm with one of his admirers, to Elmer.

On the way home, Tilly snuggled up next to her husband.

"Susan is STILL very cute isn't she?" asked Tilly, hoping for a denial.

"Yes," laughed Elmer. "She and I had a very intimate relationship for a few years. You're lucky she didn't know anything about it!"

"I'm sorry I teased you about Buff," Tilly said. "He turned out to be a real jerk. In fact, you were the handsomest man in the room tonight. I can't wait to get naked in bed with you!"

"That's funny," chuckled Elmer. "Susan said the same thing!"

"SHE WHAT?"

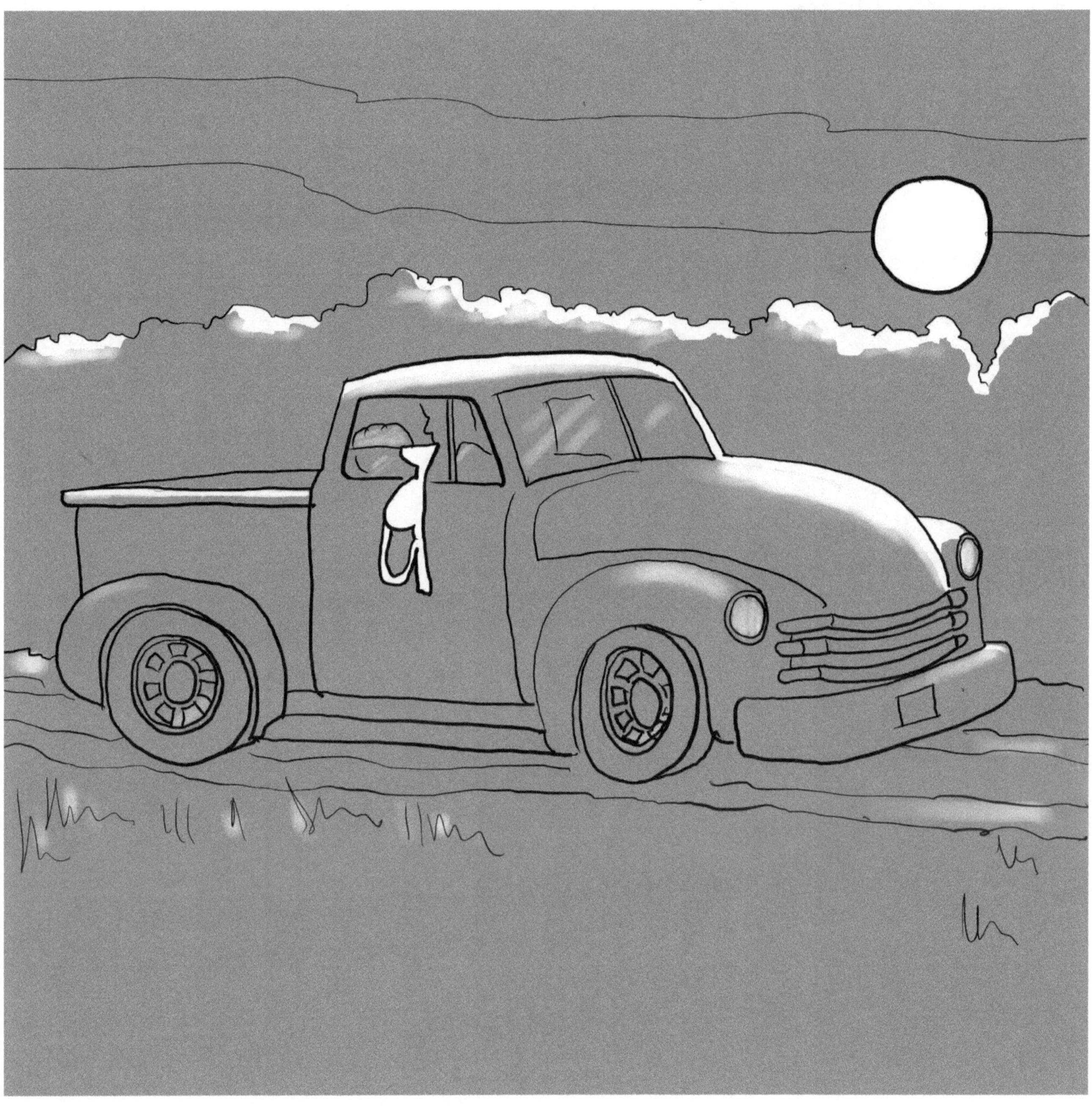

"Just teasing!" said Elmer as he gently placed his hand on Tilly's thigh.

As it had when she was eighteen, Elmer's hand on her leg caused a wave of sexual arousal to wash over Tilly. Elmer felt it at the same time.

"Elmer?"

"Yes."

"I don't think I can wait until we get home to make love to you," said Tilly.

"Well, there's always the lane behind Old Man Smith's hedgerow," suggested Elmer.

Tilly smiled. "Great idea! That's a perfect location for our personal fiftieth reunion. Do you still remember all those romantic moves you made on me when we used to park there back in high school?"

"Of course!" grinned Elmer. "In fact, I've been going over them in my mind all evening!"

Skinny-Dipping Scandal

A promising summer morning turns into an afternoon of viscous debauchery when an oblivious Tilly and Elmer find themselves unexpectedly flushed into a whirlpool of depravity. This epic story flows over sun drenched skin, cascades across naked bodies splashed with torrents of natural fluids, spurts over copious juices massaged into secret places, and meanders silently around inundated lovers. Warm, golden hued, but repulsive liquids are splattered onto bare flesh and unwisely consumed. Human emissions dribble down unwilling faces and drip from silent lips. Young fingers produce a gush of hot nectar to be swallowed in spite of rumored health risks. Trans fat saturated products flood undammed into eager, unclothed bellies. The shocking mortification of the ending will have you clutching your throat and reaching for the gin and Pepto-Bismol.

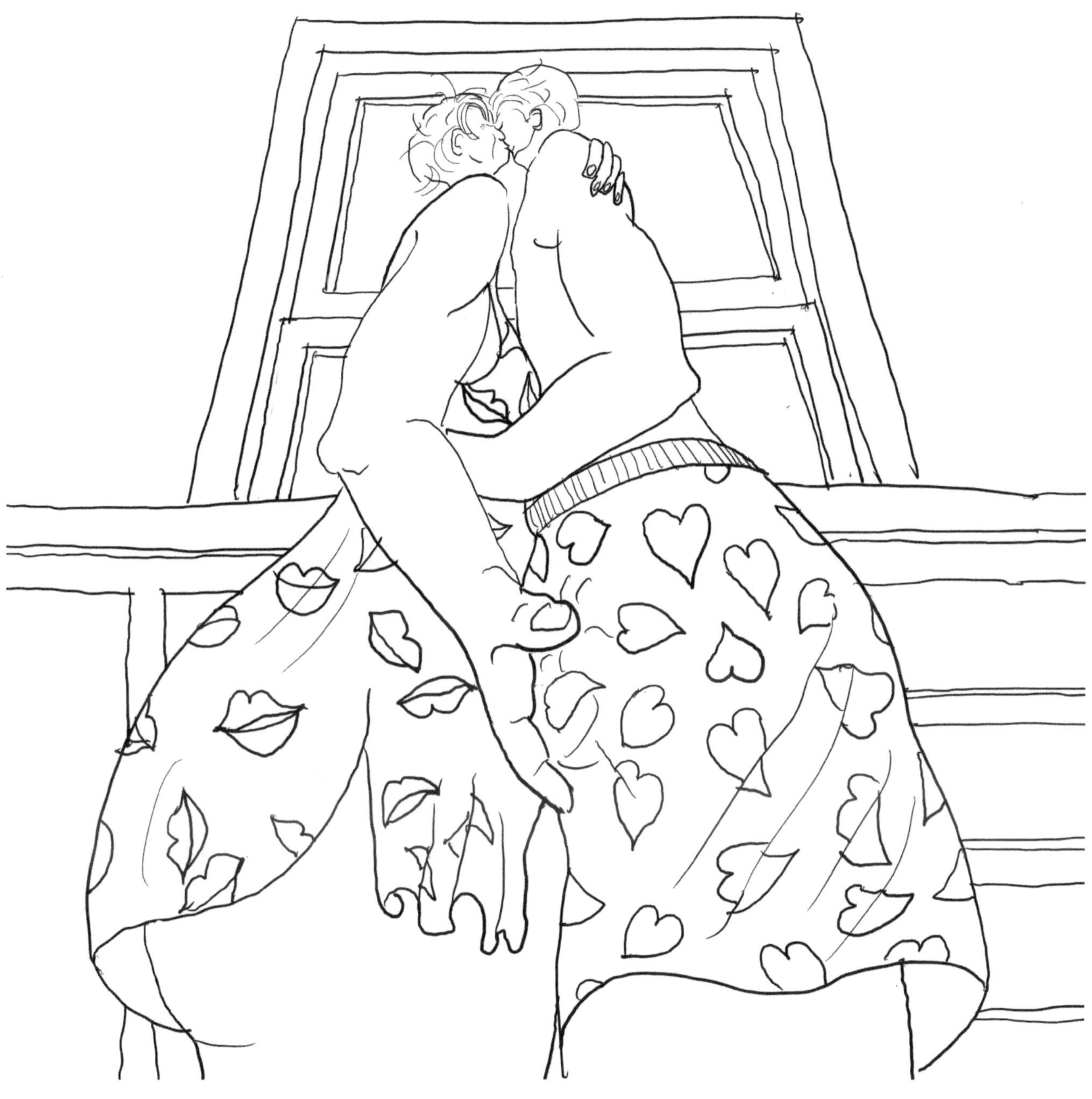

“Wake up Elmer! It’s a spectacular summer Saturday outside!” called Tilly from the kitchen.

Elmer could smell the coffee and a glance out the window confirmed Tilly’s assertion. Elmer wandered into the kitchen, still in his underwear. Tilly put her arms around him and gave him a long romantic kiss. “What’s gotten into you?” he asked.

“Nothing so far,” she said, rubbing her hand over the front of his boxers. “But I hope that will change pretty soon. Doesn’t this kind of day make you feel eighteen again? Let's go down by the creek for a 'picnic'! ”

“Can we have breakfast first?”

“Yes, I want you to be at full strength and we might forget to eat once we get there.”

“So we’re going on a SEXY picnic, are we? Maybe we can eat in between times, just like we used to,” laughed Elmer.

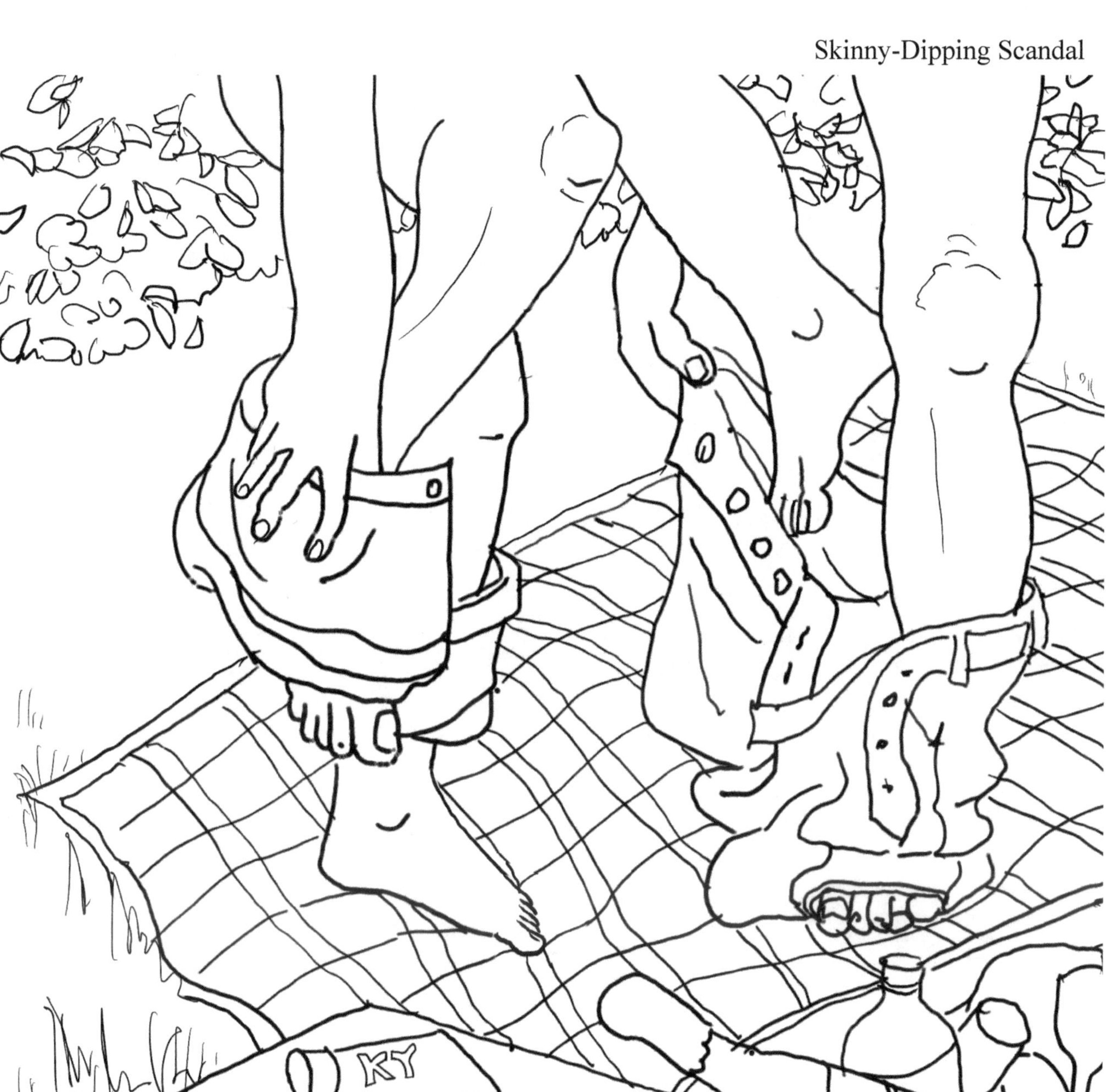

The day was reminiscent of the summer days they had spent together as teenagers, and, except for the occasional reminder caused by an aching knee or clumsy step, they might as well have been eighteen again. They laid the blanket on the soft grass under the oak tree and stashed the picnic basket in the shade. Laughing like adolescents, they got undressed in the clearing, throwing their clothes over the trunk of a downed tree. The warm sun felt delicious on their bare skin, and the vaguely sexy smell of summer in the Midwest filled the air. They were sweating from their walk, and the cool water felt refreshing as they carefully waded into the pool. Before long they were having a wonderful time splashing and teasing each other, taking time out now and then for a romantic embrace.

Their watery foreplay, however, masked the sounds of someone approaching the clearing across the creek. By the time they heard voices the interlopers were about to reach the opposite clearing where Elmer and Tilly would be fully visible in all their glory.

Truck Tryst

Tilly and Elmer decide to liven up their sex life by making love in Elmer's old truck like they did as teenagers. Unfortunately, they aren't teenagers any longer. When Elmer hurts his back in the process, Tilly, a former nurse, has to use unorthodox methods of treatment, which he enjoys as much as if their original idea had been successful.

From its opening revelation at an innocent card party, *Truck Tryst* is a riveting look at an afternoon that changed the evening plans, and perhaps their plans for many evenings to come, for a couple of sixty eight year old Midwesterners. Tilly and Elmer embark on a dangerous expedition, the unlikely vehicle for which is a 1952 Chevy pick up truck which remains parked in the driveway throughout the trip. Even though the journey covers no distance at all, along the way we learn about concession, limberness lost, misfortune, and the power of love to make everything feel good in the end.

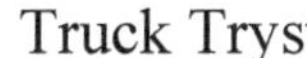

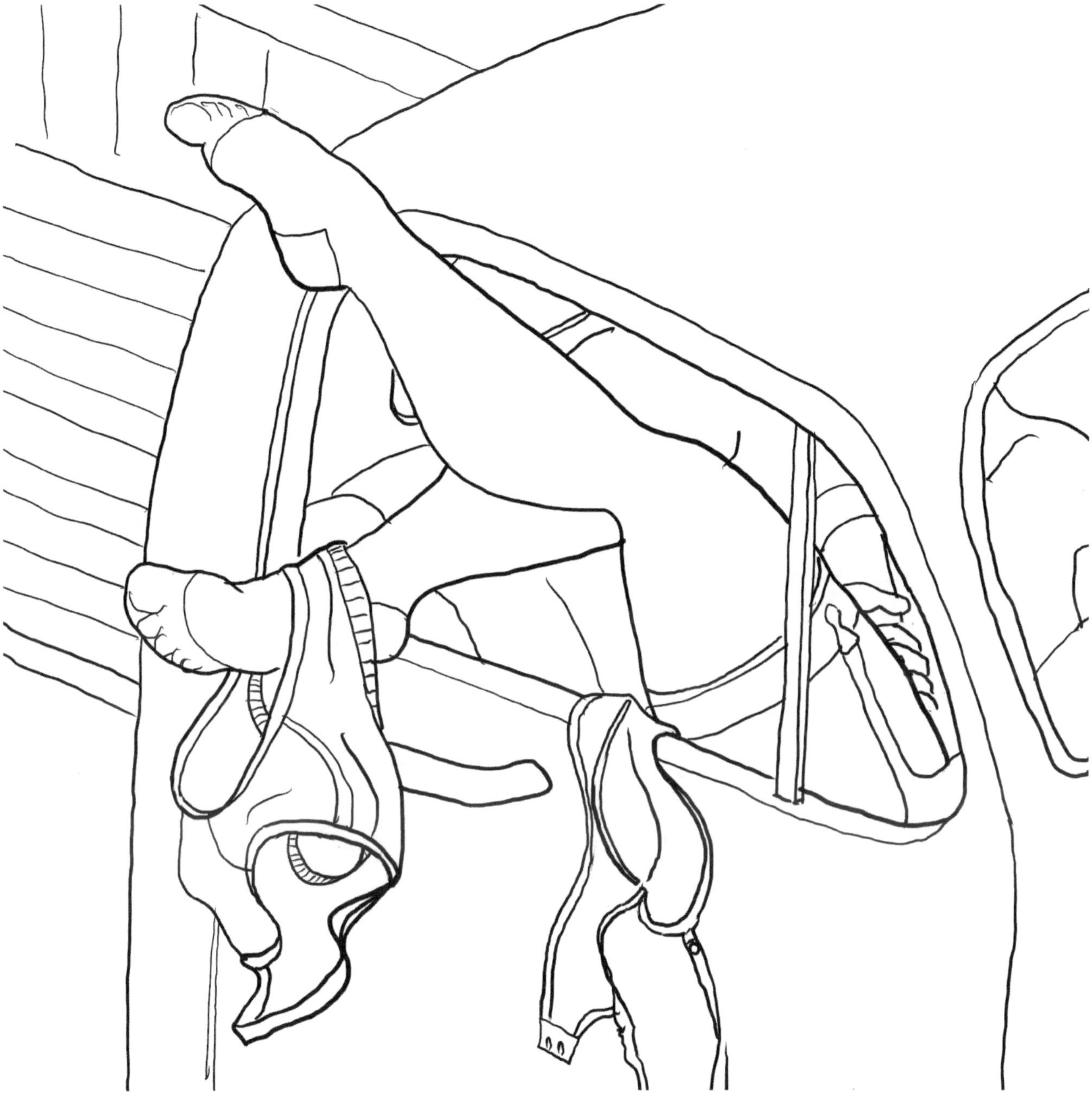

"Come on, Elmer, let's give that old truck a workout tonight like we used to."

"OK, Tilly, I'll do it with you in the truck on two conditions," said Elmer.

"OK, I won't lean back against the horn again like that one time," promised Tilly.

"I guess that makes three conditions," laughed Elmer. "Can we just drive the truck up behind the house? I don't want to be out in somebody's pasture when we do it."

"Ok, if you're chicken, I guess I can live with that. What's the other condition?"

"You have to dress up like you did when we used to do it in the truck. Tight sweater, skirt with those puffy slip things…"

"Crinolines."

"Right, crinolines. And white cotton panties, garter belt, stockings. The full regalia."

"You hated that stuff at the time; it took too long to get it off!" Tilly reminded him.

"Well, I love it now. And I have all the time in the world to get it off, to coin a phrase. Is it a deal?"

Tilly's Afternoon Delight

In this sizzling story of summer in the Midwest, Gene Clements has written the hottest Tilly and Elmer yet. Elmer and his friend Eddie go fishing in hopes of keeping cool on a hot Iowa afternoon, while Tilly plans to enjoy the heat by reading a pornographic novel. Her afternoon gets even hotter when Johnson, a young arborist, comes to trim the oak tree in her backyard. Tilly's offer of a cold gin and tonic fails to cool things off, and by the end of the afternoon, things have gotten hotter, wetter, and stickier than she expected. Not that she has any complaints, at least until the morning after, when she has to replant the bed of maidenhair ferns next to the garage.

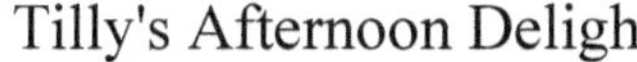

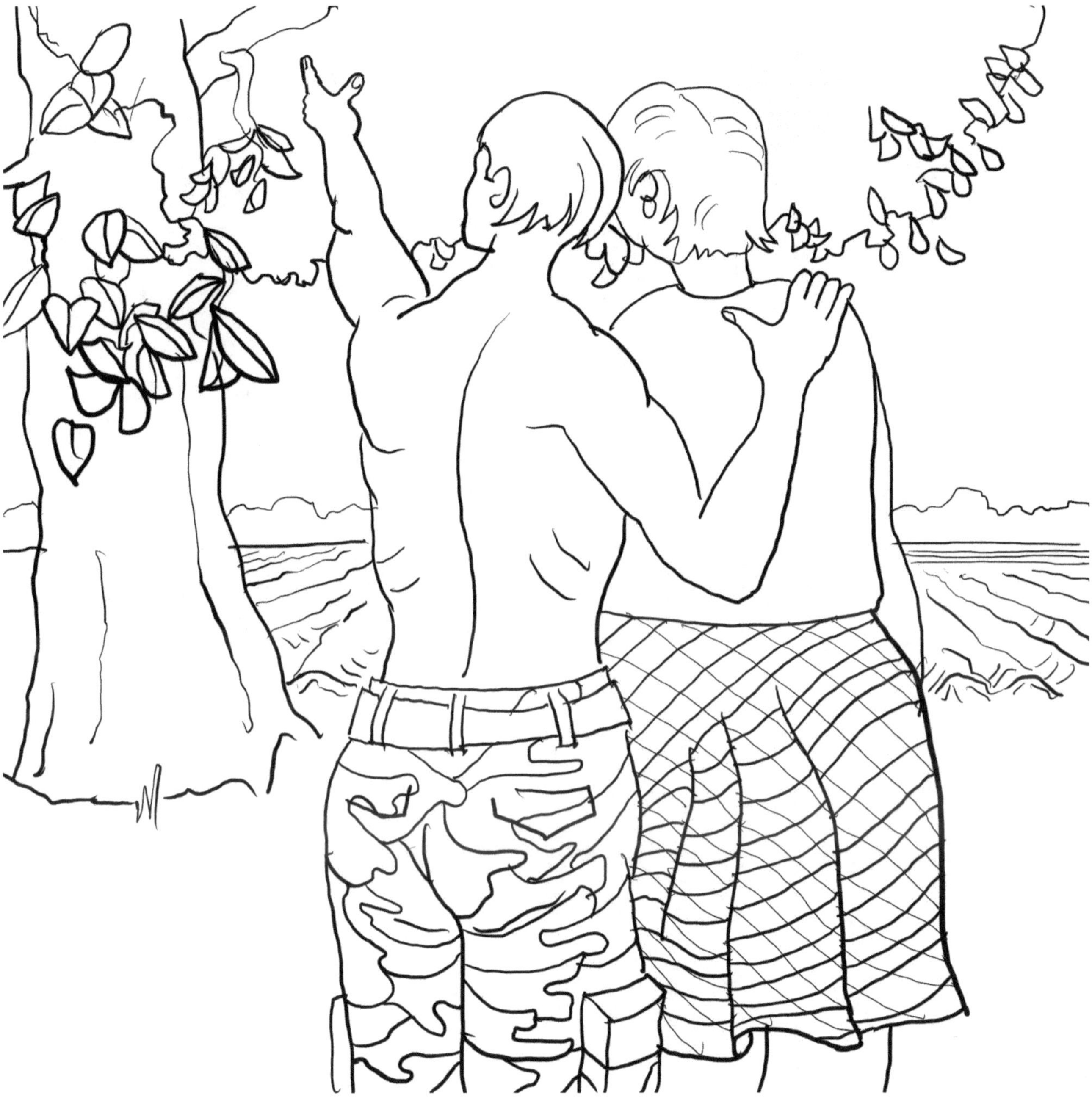

"It's so hot, I'm going to make myself a gin and tonic," Tilly said to Johnson. "Would you like one before you get started?"

"Oh no, Mrs. Talbot. Not now," Johnson said. "Maybe when I'm done climbing." Tilly was convinced he was trying to look down her top when he said it.

"Suit yourself. There's plenty of refreshment available whenever you want it."

Tilly went inside, fixed a tall gin and tonic, and got her iPad. She decided it was too hot to wear a bra all afternoon, so she took hers off and left an extra button undone when she put her shirt back on. When she got back outside, Johnson was already at the top of the tree, attaching a safety rope to an upper branch. His movements in the tree gave her an unusual perspective, looking up at his muscular legs spread across two branches and his buttocks encased in the tight shorts, which were becoming damp with sweat.

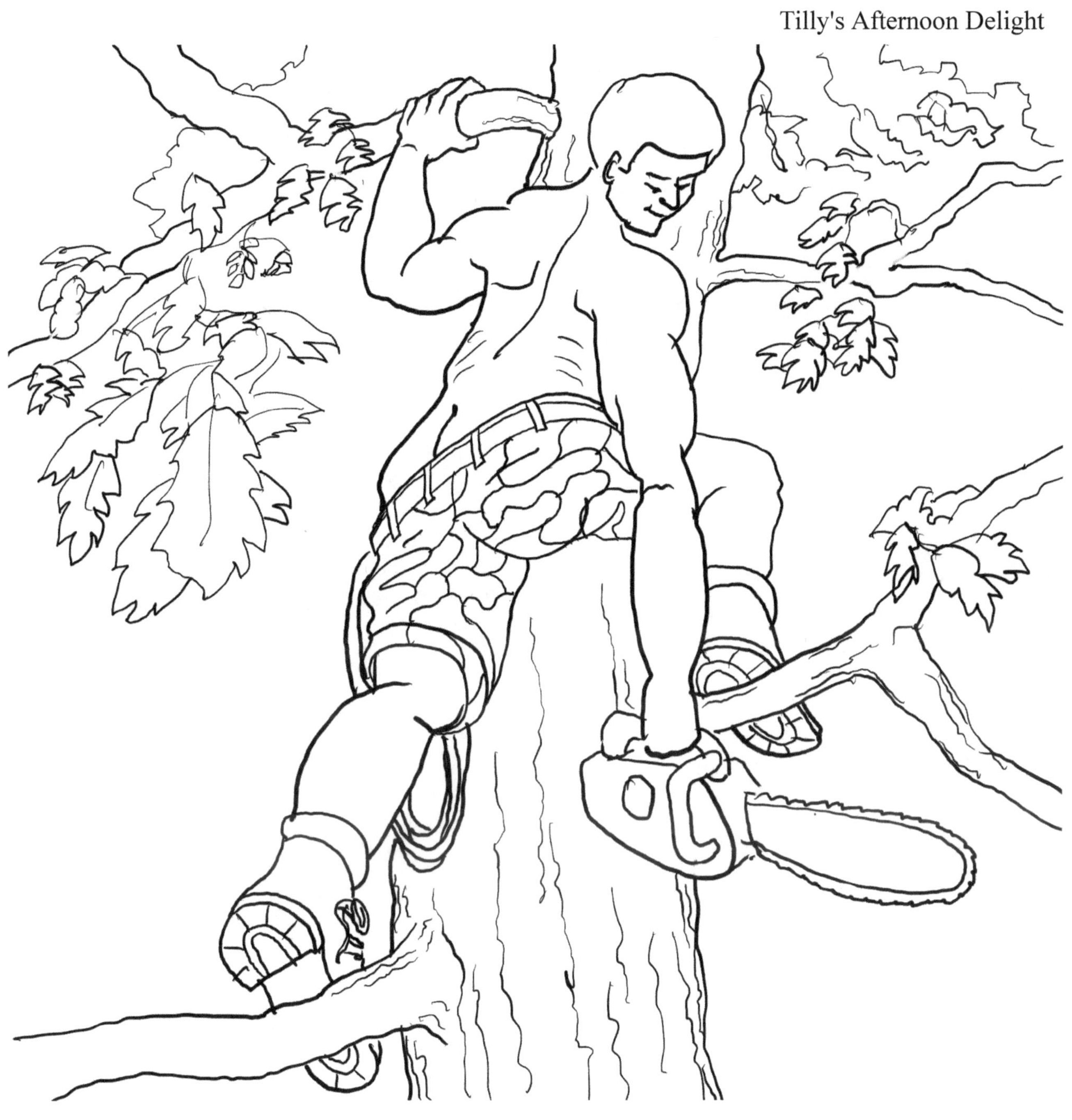

Tilly took another sip of her gin and tonic, and was surprised to find the glass empty when she finished.

She lay back and watched Johnson, seemingly without a care in the world, risking life and limb as he moved gracefully from branch to branch like a wild animal. She closed her eyes for a minute and let the memories of lazy, romantic, delicious summer afternoons, when something exciting was bound to happen, wash over her. Tilly imagined Johnson as a ballet dancer or a gymnast, effortlessly moving his body to present a series of beautiful shapes in the treetop. The air was still, with only an occasional slight breeze to remind her of the stillness. Heat waves rose from the field west of the house. A tickle of sweat trickled down between Tilly's breasts. The areas where her skirt or skin touched the chair were wet with sweat. Insects buzzed in the bed of ferns along the north wall of the garage.

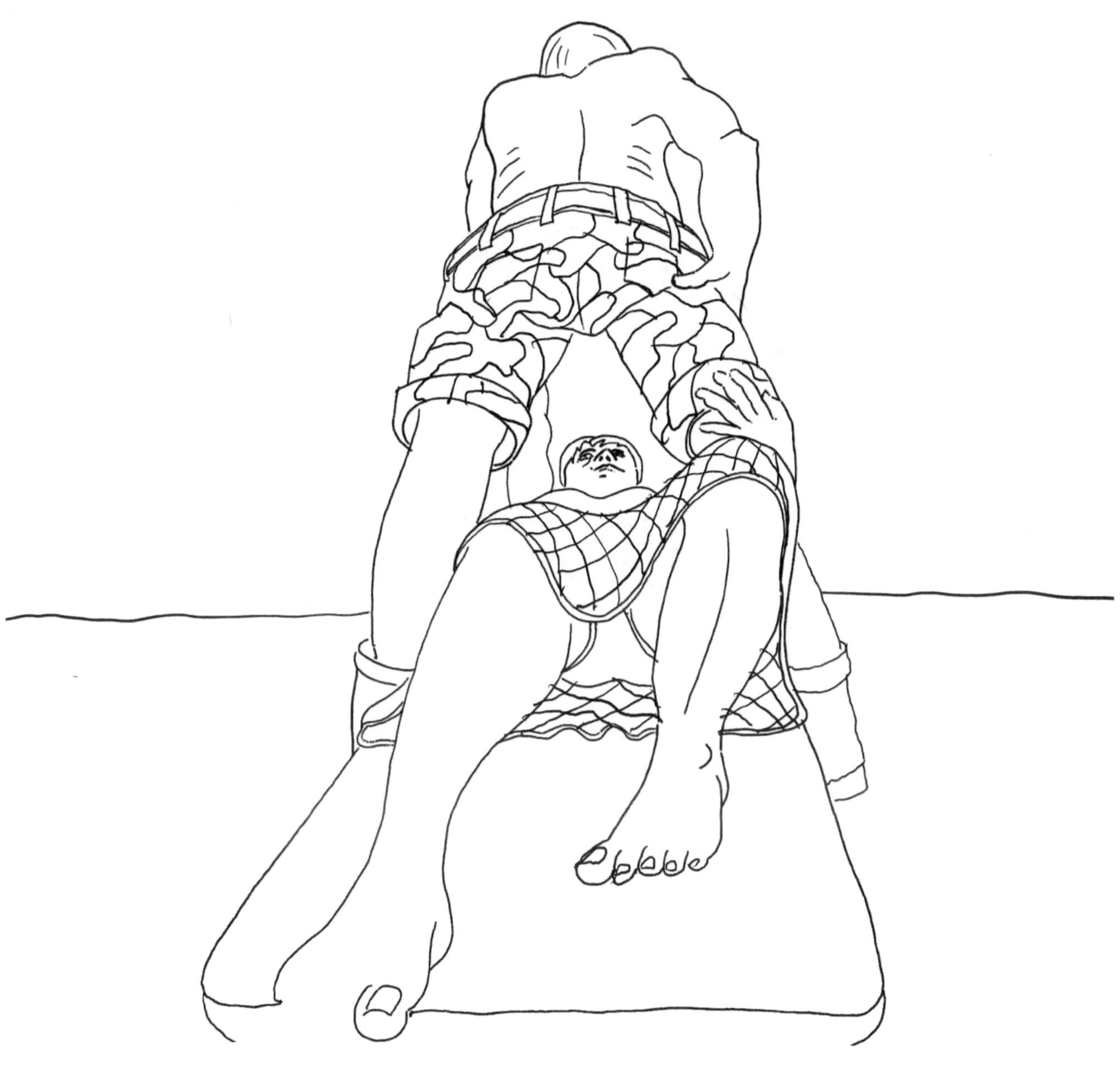

"Are you ready for that gin and tonic?"

"You bet!" he said, pulling a lawn chair up next to her beach chair, which she began to think of as more of a bed than a chair.

"Could you get it sweetheart?" Tilly asked, a little unsteadily. "The fixings are on the counter in the kitchen."

"Sure!" said Johnson. "Do you want another one?"

"I want a big stiff one," said Tilly, starting to giggle after she realized how that had come out.

He brought the drinks and they talked about his work and how exciting it must be to climb trees for a living. Tilly revealed that she was an expert tree climber as a kid, but hadn't tried it for years.

"There's really nothing to it," said Johnson. "You could climb that tree as well as me with a little help."

"Come on!" he said, standing up and taking her hand.

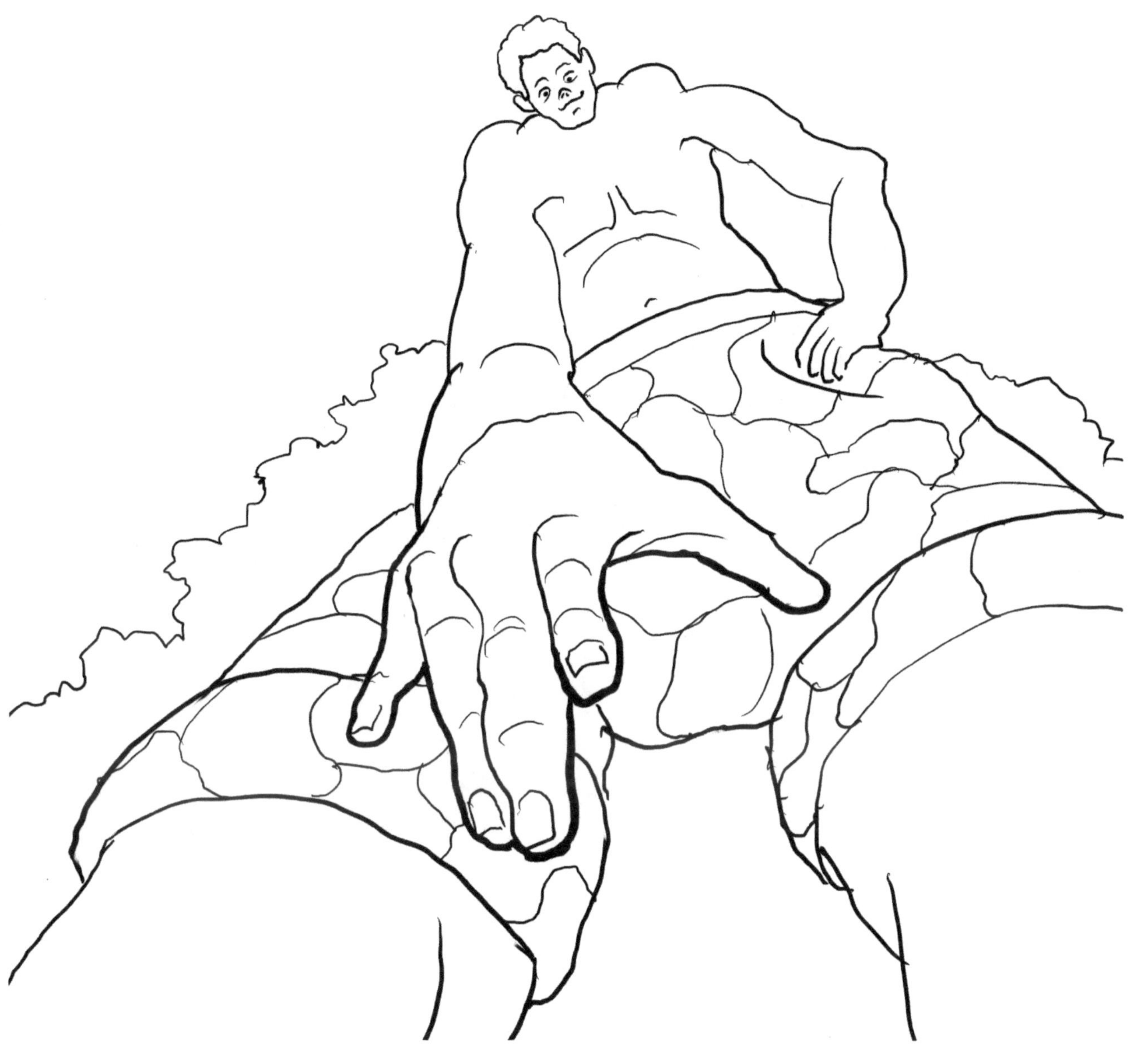

He lifted Tilly up onto a low branch. Even though there was no breeze, the tree seemed to be swaying. After a few minutes he reached up, put his strong hands on her waist and slid her off the branch toward him. Tilly was a little off balance and put her feet out in front of her as he did so, catching her toes in the waistband of his shorts and pushing them down to his ankles as he lowered her into his arms. He kicked them off and carried her back to the beach chair where he laid her gently onto her back.

Again he was towering over her, solid as the oak tree he had just been working on. Tilly tried to focus her eyes. "It's so big!" she said, dreamily.

A hand touched her inner thigh.

"What's so big?" said Elmer, leaning over her.

"Johnson's...," said Tilly, squinting as she looked up. "Elmer?"

"Of course, who else? Johnson's what was so big, his bill for the tree? How much was it?"

Tilly and Elmer In - Decent Exposure

As she does every fall, Tilly begins to worry that she and Elmer are getting into a boring routine and resolves to find some new adventures to get them out of it. Her plan this time is to take an acting class at the local community college. She convinces Elmer to join her in her academic pursuits by signing up for a yoga class. When she is cast as an expert kisser in the class play and Elmer's yoga instructor asks him to pose for her artist's drawing group however, each begins to wonder whether they are getting a little too far out of their old routine.

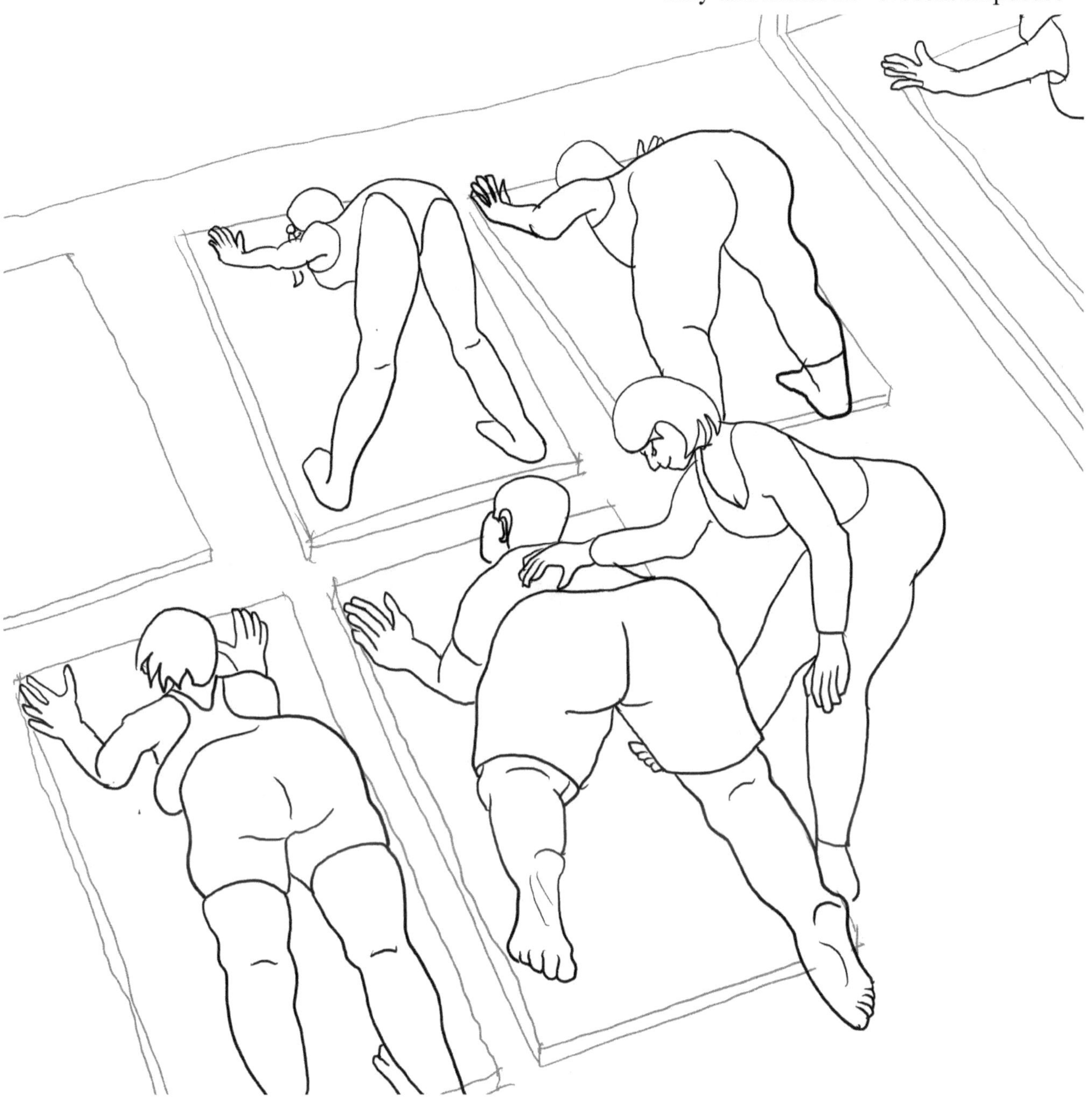

"You should sign up for a course too, Elmer. It's time we got out of our boring routine," said Tilly.

This declaration was part of their boring routine. Toward the end of every summer, without fail, Tilly began to feel that everyone else in South Branch was living an exciting and adventurous life and that she and Elmer were letting the world pass them by.

"I wouldn't know what to sign up for," he said warily.

"I'll look for something that's at the same time as the acting class I'm thinking about," Tilly offered, thumbing through the class schedule. "How about a yoga class? Here's one at 7:30 every Tuesday and Thursday evening. That would be perfect!"

"I don't know anything about yoga," he said.

"That's the IDEA Elmer; if you knew about it you wouldn't need a class. You should try it. We might even be able to get back into some of our old favorite bedtime 'postures' if you get what I mean!"

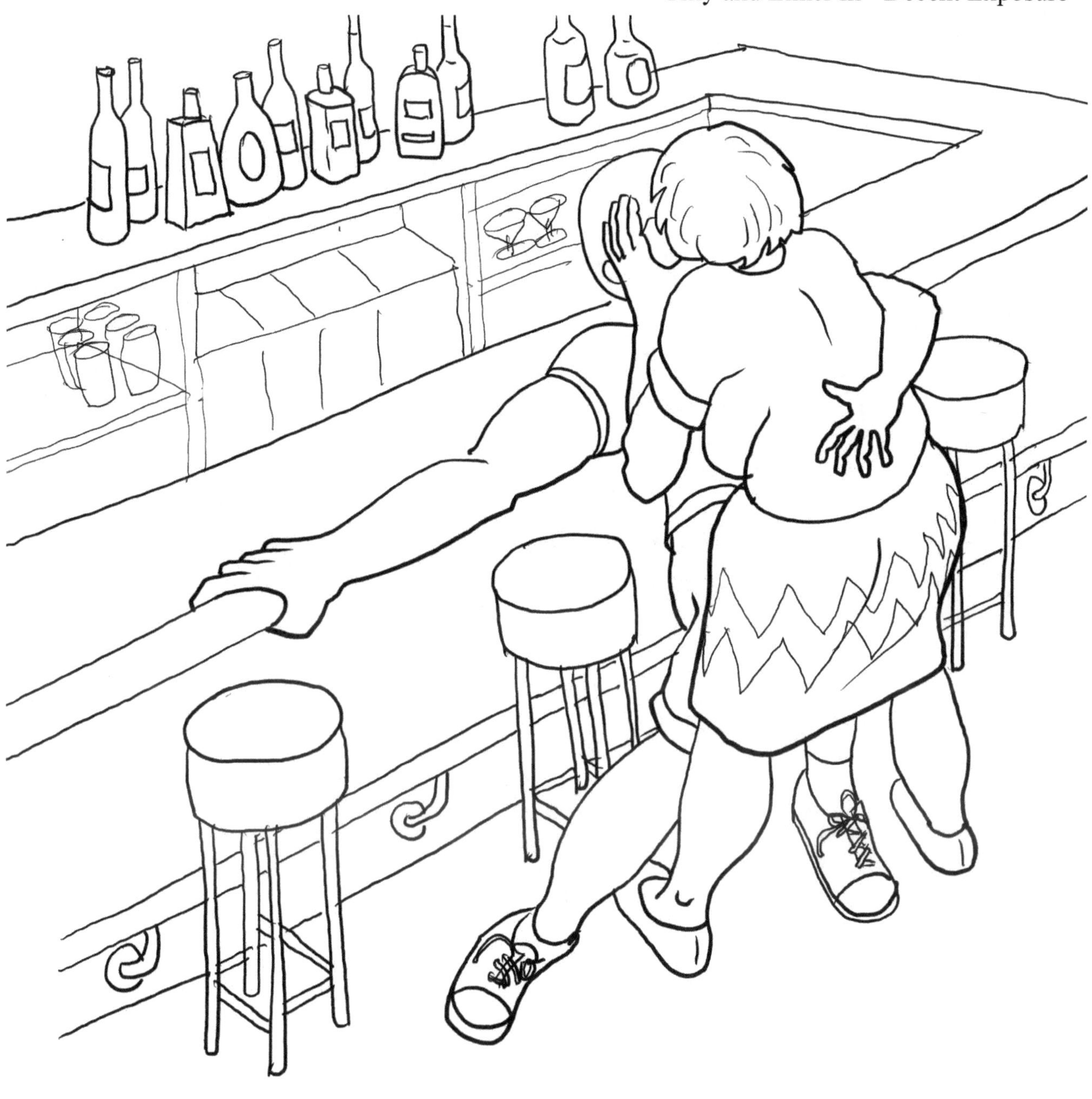

Tilly plays the title role in ***Mrs. Abbott's Awesome Afternoon***

MRS. ABBOTT the proprietor of Pete's Pub

(Laughing) If I were forty years younger, I'd show you!

TOM a college student

I don't care how old you are. I'm desperate. I'm going to lose my girlfriend if I don't get better at this stupid kissing thing.

(Mrs. Abbott looks at Tom for a minute, annoyed by his cluelessness. Then, without a word she slowly folds her towel, turns her back to Tom, and hangs it on a hook behind the bar. She unhurriedly takes a bottle of Old Granddad from the back bar and pours a shot which she downs in a gulp. She noisily sets down the empty glass, then walks around the end of the bar, stopping in front of Tom. She looks down at his face for a moment, regarding his look of bewilderment.)

MRS. ABBOTT

Stupid kissing thing, huh? We'll see about that!

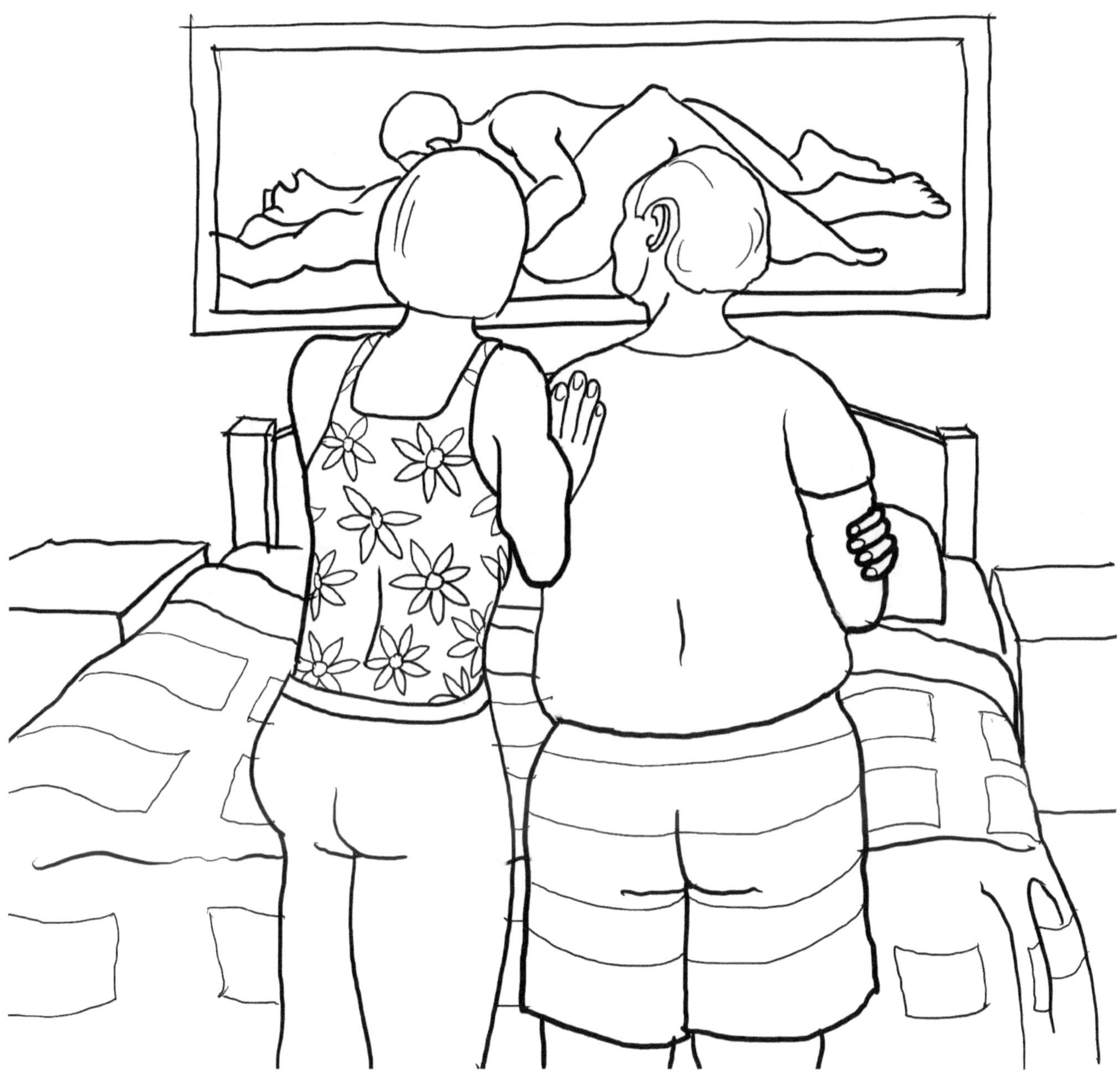

"Elmer, would you consider modeling for my drawing group?" Arlene asked. "It would be a lot of fun to draw you. What do you think?"

...

Apparently Arlene was the patron of a talented artist who always drew nudes, either alone or posed in groups. Some of the drawings bordered on the erotic; some, especially those displayed in her bedroom, were on the other side of the border. Elmer inquired as to the identity of the artist.

"I did all those of course," she said laughing. "I couldn't afford to buy all this art from any real artist."

"You must be a real artist," Elmer said. "These are really um, interesting!"

"Thank you!" Arlene said. "Some models just arouse the artist in me."

She lightly touched his arm.

Suddenly, an obvious fact hit Elmer like a bolt of lightning; he wasn't going to be modeling in his yoga gear! Arlene and four strangers expected him to pose for them totally naked!

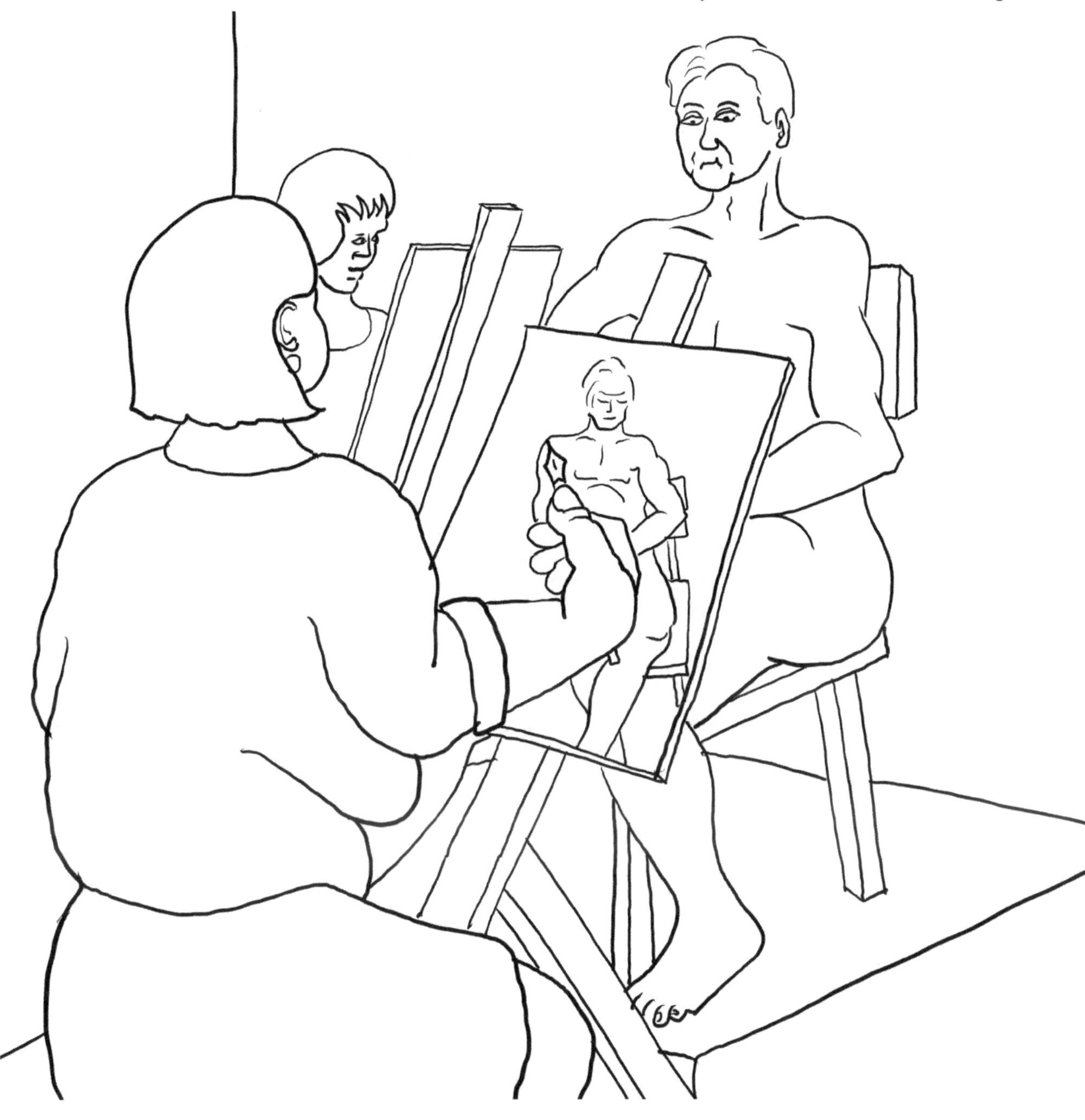

"What's the matter, Elmer?" Arlene asked.

"Um," Elmer said, unable to take his eyes off one of Arlene's more risqué drawings.

"You did understand that we always draw our models nude didn't you?" she asked.

"No," Elmer admitted. "I guess I thought it would be just like yoga class."

Arlene looked at him and grasped his upper arm.

Speaking softly, she said, "It will be fine, Elmer. Remember, no one is allowed to feel any stress over his performance. Anyway, we've all seen naked men before and I can assure you we'll be too busy trying to produce a decent drawing to critique your physique. Contrary to the common perception we will be trying to capture something elusive on paper rather than engaging in unbridled voyeurism. All you have to do is relax and try to hold still."

This seemed impossible, but Elmer found her proclamation a little reassuring, which was especially welcome since he didn't feel it would be possible to back out at this late date. He would just have to grin and bear it, or more accurately, bare it. He smiled at his unintended joke.

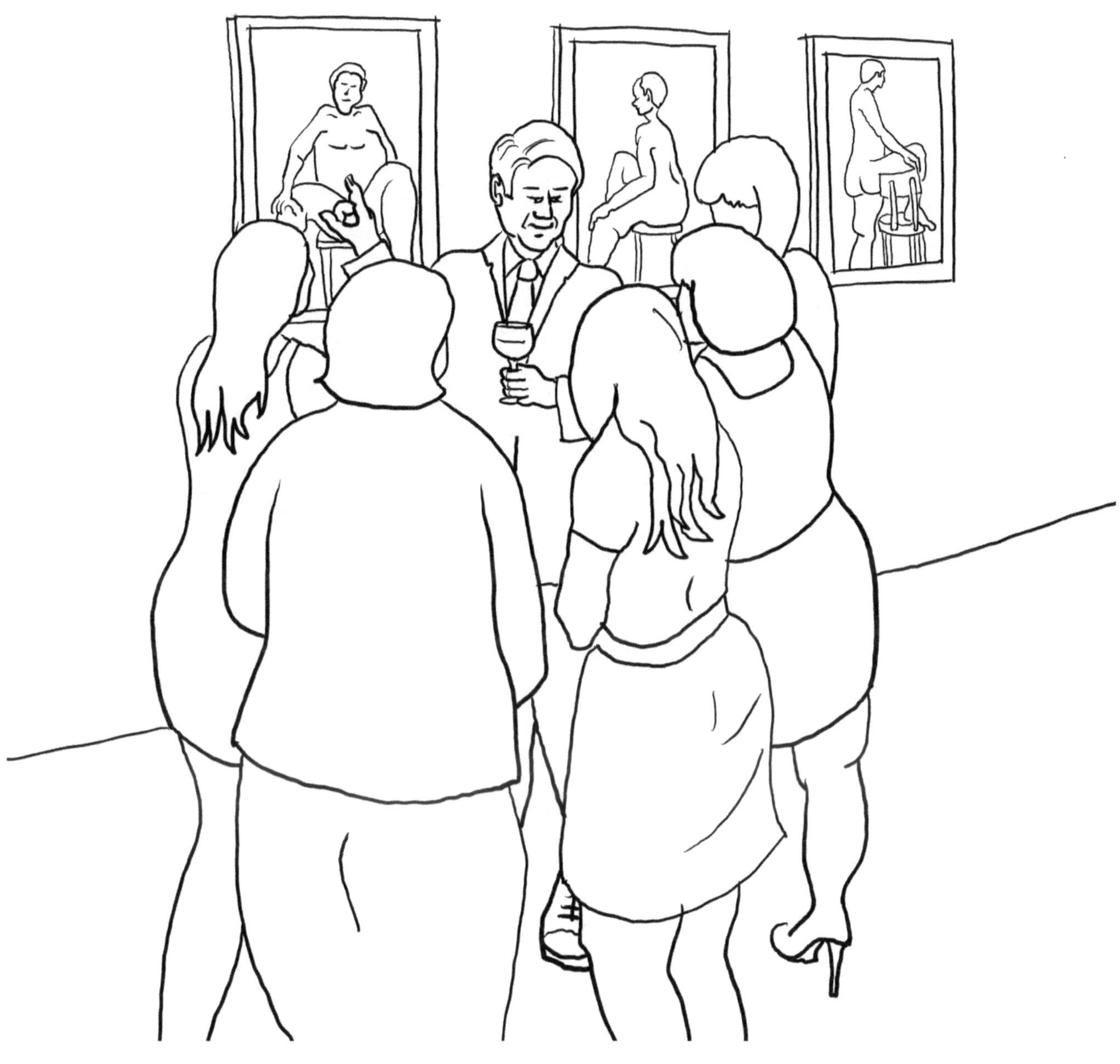

"It looks like we'll both be stars before long," Elmer told Tilly when he got home.

"What do you mean?"

"I'm to be featured in a major art show downtown the same weekend as your performance in *Mrs. Abbott's Awesome Afternoon*. We'll be the talk of the town!"

"The gossip of the town is more like it. This is starting to get out of hand, Elmer!"

"Look Tilly, I can't help it if my naked body is a sensation," he said. "You'll be the talk of the town too after the play. I guess famous couples like us just have to learn to put up with that kind of adulation."

Tilly and Elmer attended the gallery opening where they spent the evening sipping too much wine and discussing "balance", "negative space", and "gestures", with art lovers who didn't know what those terms meant either.

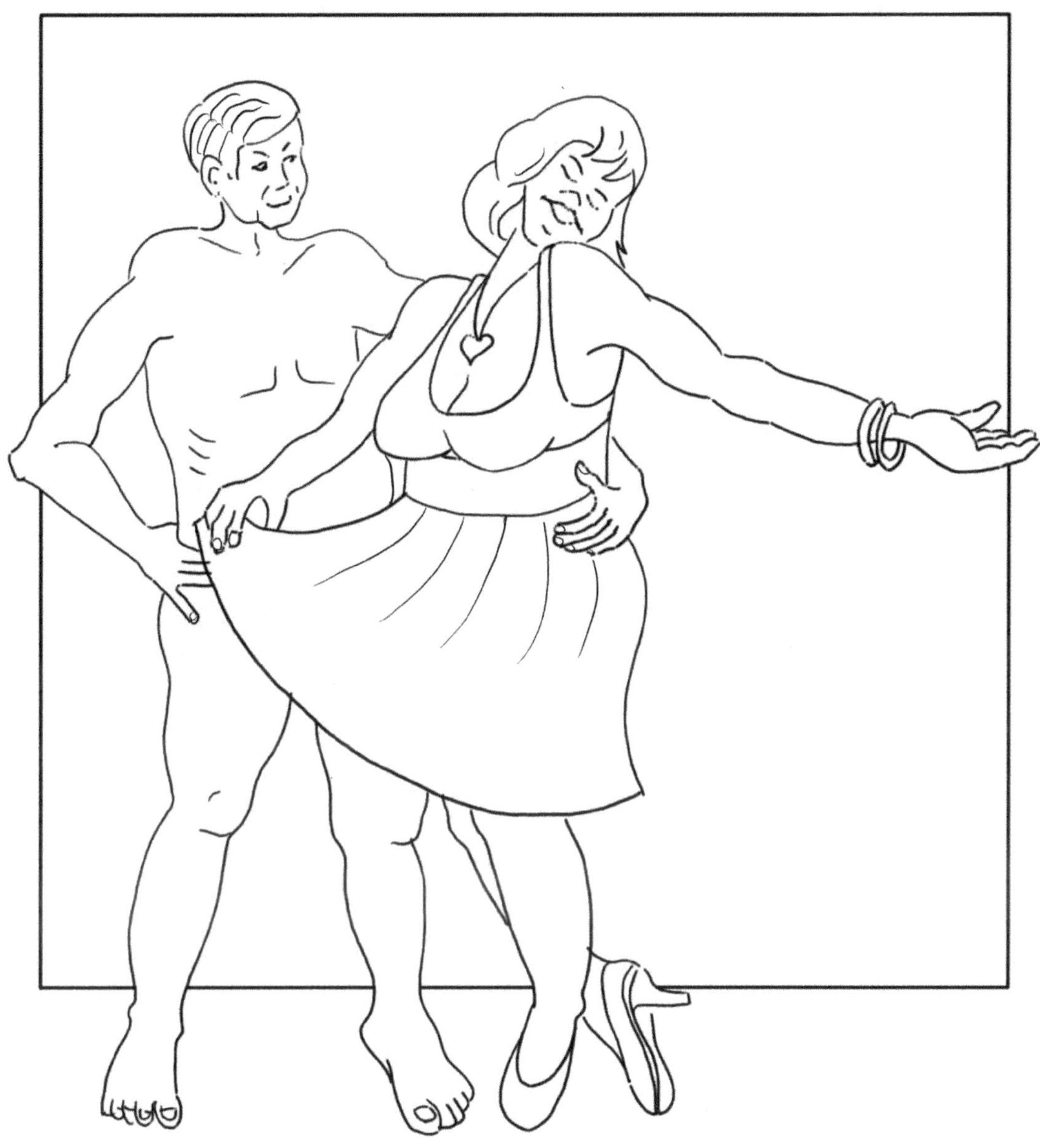

"Tilly Talbot of South Branch steals the show as Mrs. Abbott. By the end, every man in the audience, including this reviewer, wanted to sign up for some of her kissing lessons.

"We're looking forward to seeing Mrs. Talbot in future performances, or at least as the star attraction in the 'Kissing Booth' at the county fair next summer, and I'm sure there would be no shortage of students if she were to begin giving private lessons."

Tilly promptly clipped out the article, found a frame for it, and hung it over the bed next to Elmer's "likeness". As they stood looking at the two documents, Elmer quietly disrobed and Tilly gave him a rocket-launching kiss.

"Tilly?"

"Yes, Elmer."

"The next time we want to get out of our old routine, what do you say we just go on a cruise?"

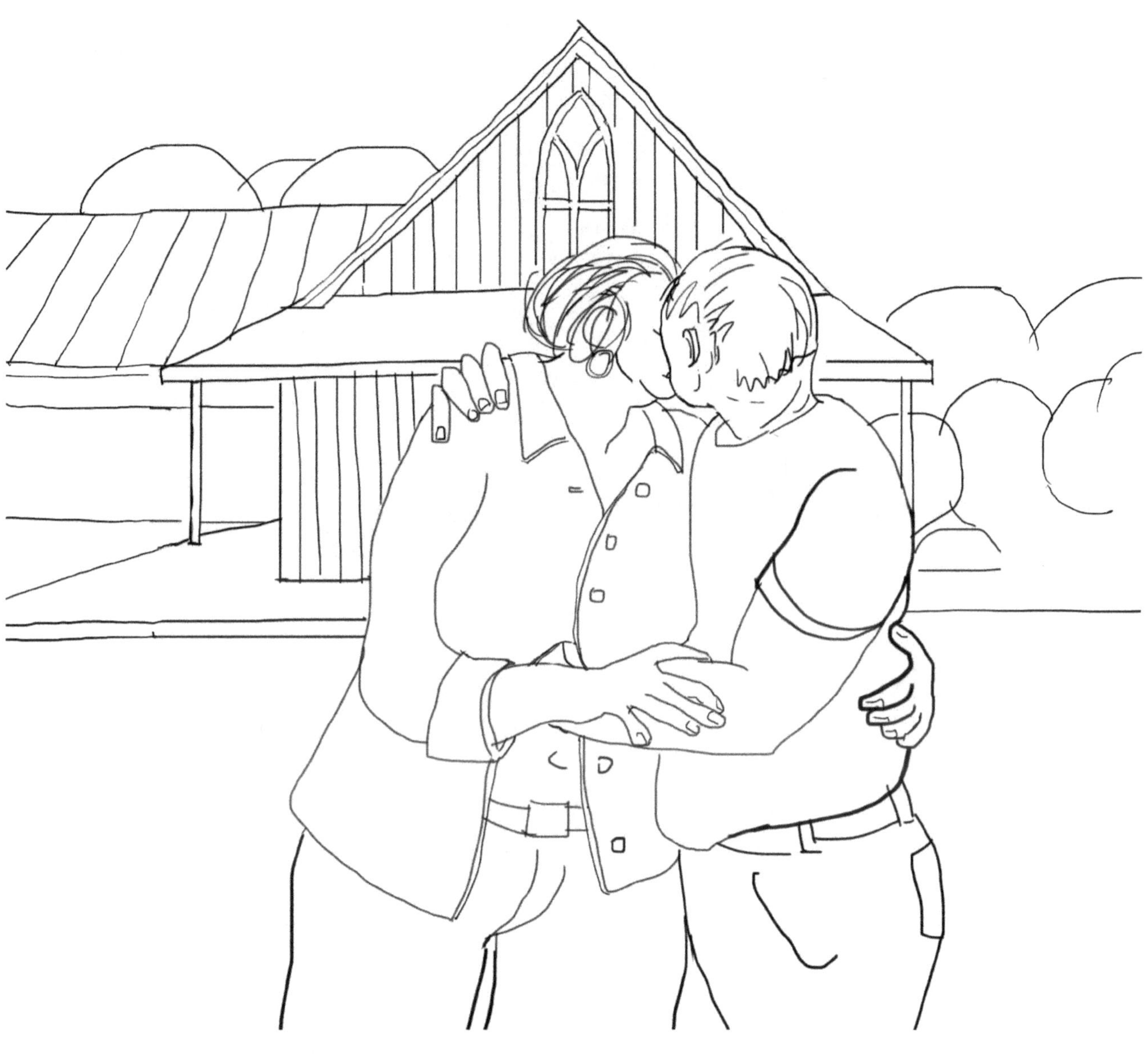

About the author:

Gene Clements is an artist, writer, architect, and educator. He grew up in the Midwest and has lived in California since the 1970's. Gene thinks he's eighteen, but like Tilly and Elmer he's reminded frequently that a half-century has passed since then.

The Tilly and Elmer series began accidently when, as a joke, Gene wrote the first couple of paragraphs of a story about a frisky older couple and then made a drawing of them. His friends thought the paragraphs and drawing were funny and wanted to know how the story ended. Now, for better or worse they know, or at least they will if Tilly and Elmer ever let Gene stop writing about them.

TILLY AND ELMER TITLES:

• ***Tilly and Elmer - The Sexy Seniors of South Branch***. The full collection of short stories recounting Tilly and Elmer's grownup adventures is available in **paperback** at CreateSpace, Amazon, and other retailers and as an e-book at the Apple iBooks Store, Amazon, Smashwords, Barnes and Noble and other retailers. The short stories in this series are also available individually at any of the e-book retailers above:

Tilly and Elmer Get Crazy
Tilly and Elmer go to Las Vegas
Skinny-Dipping Scandal
Tilly's Afternoon Delight
Tilly and Elmer Get Warmed Up
Tilly and Elmer's 50th Class Reunion
Truck Tryst
Tilly and Elmer in - Decent Exposure

• ***The Sexy Seniors of South Branch Coloring Book*** (this book)

• ***Tilly and Elmer FlashbackX - Coming of Age in South Branch***. In this sweet, nostalgic, funny, and sometimes erotic book, Tilly and Elmer, a frisky couple from South Branch, Iowa, recount their romantic and awkward high school dating years, from their first date, in 1961, through the night they finally went "all the way", to their heart wrenching departures for distant colleges in 1963. If you grew up in the 1950's or 60's, you may find these stories sounding a little familiar as Tilly and Elmer reveal the clumsy interactions, the shocking miscommunication, and the catastrophes that seem funny in retrospect, as well as the surprising delights and breathtaking pleasures of learning about sex and falling hopelessly in love in an age when "sex ed." was all do it yourself and taught through hands on experience.

Coming of Age in South Branch is available in **paperback** and as an e-book at the locations noted above.

Chapter 1 Is That Your Thigh I'm Squeezing?
Chapter 2 Falling for a Kiss
Chapter 3 Punch Drunk on Love
Chapter 4 The Breast Laid Plans
Chapter 5 Prom Night and Spanish Olives
Chapter 6 Skinny-Dipping Naked with No Clothes On
Chapter 7 Emission Accomplished
Chapter 8 The First "First Time"
Chapter 9 Strokes of Luck
Chapter 10 The Coming of Spring
Chapter 11 Wide Awake at the Sleeptite Motel

• ***The Coming of Age in South Branch Coloring Book*** **-** Coming Soon

---

Find out more about Tilly and Elmer at TillyandElmer.com

Illustrations from ***Tilly and Elmer FlashbackX - Coming of Age in South Branch***

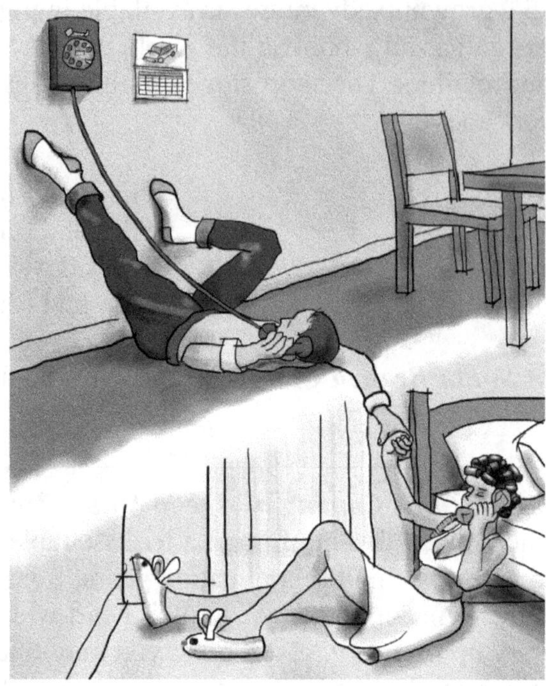

The telephone, Chapter 3, "Punch Drunk on Love"

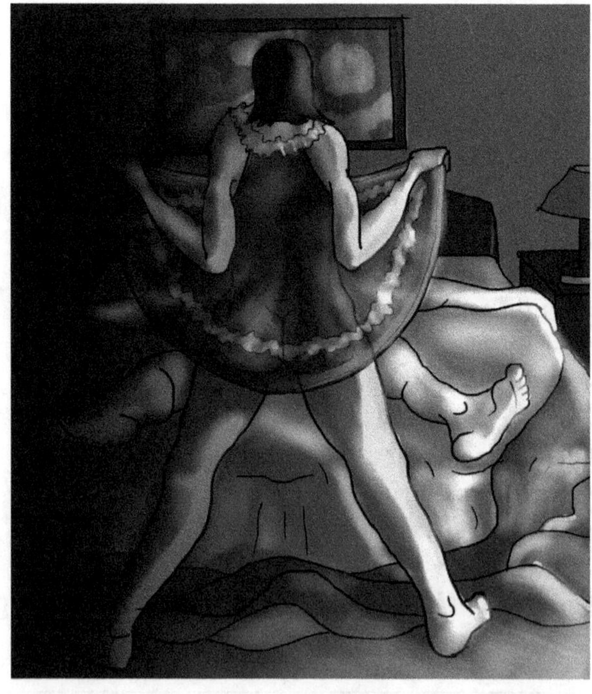

Baby doll pajamas, Chapter 11, "Wide Awake at the Sleeptite Motel"

www.ingramcontent.com/pod-product-compliance
Lightning Source LLC
LaVergne TN
LVHW081422110826
845149LV00010B/1841

* 9 7 8 0 9 9 6 2 8 2 7 2 7 *